Side Hustle to Full Time Income:

From $0 to $100k per Month with Retail and Online Arbitrage

By Jimmy Smith

Foreword by Jim Cockrum, Internet Entrepreneur and Host of the Podcast *Silent Sales Machine Radio*

Download the Audiobook Free!!

READ THIS FIRST

To say thank you for downloading my book, I would like to give you the audiobook version 100% FREE!!

I know you're more likely to finish this book if you have the audiobook. I even narrated the book myself so it will feel like we are having a conversation (and I threw in some extra thoughts along the way!!)

Since this book has some visual elements to it, I wanted you to be able to have both the written and audio options when needed.

Instead of paying $10-$20 for the audiobook, I'd like to give it to you for free…

askjimmysmith.com/audiobook

Free Video Summary and Jumpstart Course!!

Want a free video summary of this book to get you making progress on YOUR Amazon business quickly?

Check out this video training and overview of the process.

In this training I cover 3 main things:

1. How to successfully launch your Amazon business
2. How to find profitable, consistent products with examples and live walk-throughs
3. How to scale your business so you can focus on the important revenue growth tasks

Surprise Bonus Content Included!!

askjimmysmith.com/jumpstart

Bonus Book Resources

You'll find *all* resources mentioned throughout this book at the following web address:

askjimmysmith.com/bookresources

All the Google sheets, templates, Standard Operating Procedures, plus any supplies you'll ever need are there. In addition, I've included easy links to any and all software and course suggestions that matter to you, the replens seller.

Be sure to check out my website at askjimmysmith.com or follow me on my Youtube Channel @AskJimmySmith

OVER 1,000 SUCCESS STORIES!!

Believe it or not, the content in this book has led to over 1,000 success stories since I came out with the original course in July of 2019.

When we started I had no idea it would lead to this type of consistent success and I'm so thankful that God has used this information to bless so many people to have businesses ranging from $10,000 per month to $300,000+ per month using the strategies in this book (which is based on the original course).

Now I know this is hard to believe (even for me!) which is why I put together a page where you can freely see over 500 of them. Use this as a motivator to read through this book and apply the concepts taught.

askjimmysmith.com/success

Earnings Disclaimer: Please Read Before Proceeding

While all of these success stories/testimonials are from real people and we get more each and every day, please understand however that the results posted at this website and through this book are not typical. I'm not implying you'll duplicate them or that you'll get any results at all! Your results will vary greatly and will depend on many factors including your experience, work ethic and other factors as well. Business always involves risk and your best chance of success is to take consistent, intentional action. We can equip and inspire you, but no one, including me can guarantee your results!

ISBN: 979-8637445585

"There's never been a better time to be in business."

~Jim Cockrum
Silent Sales Machine

Dedication

As this is the second version of the book, I want to dedicate this to all of the thousands of people that have either gone through my courses or purchased this book in the past! We've seen well over 1,000 success stories as a result of the action you've taken. The content in this book only goes as far as you allow it to by taking action and I'm extremely humbled as to the response I've received in the last few years through your successes and thank you notes. This 2nd edition is dedicated to all of you and I'm excited to see where your business grows to moving forward!

Table of Contents

Foreword by Jim Cockrum

From my vantage point, the book you now hold is quite likely the greatest written roadmap into Amazon selling success that's available in the world. That's a big statement, but I'm about to offer you proof. This bold statement is especially true for you if you've yet to earn any significant income online because we turn "clueless newbies" into success stories more than any other trainers in the E-commerce space that I'm aware of. I've spoken firsthand directly with hundreds of people who have used the exact ideas in this book to build incredible businesses on the Amazon platform - more about that in a moment.

Since 1999 I've sold multiple tens of millions of dollars of products and services online and I've watched the entire industry mature. My twenty plus year E-commerce adventure has given me a front row seat to witness literally hundreds of business strategies and leaders rise and fall. This book is an oasis from the noise. It is with great confidence that I tell you that you've hit the jackpot with this book for two primary reasons.

First, Amazon clearly represents the lowest hanging fruit opportunity of our time when it comes to building an online business. It's inarguable. For example, Amazon continues to dominate the E-Commerce space in the US and is responsible for about 50% of all transactions online daily. New millionaires are emerging constantly from among those who have learned how to navigate the business opportunities made available by Amazon.

Next, in the sea of Amazon business options that are available to us, Jimmy has clearly identified what is almost certainly the lowest hanging fruit Amazon opportunity. We call it the "Amazon Replens" model of Amazon selling. In this book, Jimmy spells out the steps involved in methodically building a low-risk, low start-up capital, steady cash-flow business on Amazon.

And if that's not convincing enough, we've seen time and time again that mastering these relatively simple, foundational Replens strategies will open up additional, incredible doors for you to walk through as your E-commerce adventure matures.

Working closely with Jimmy for the past several years to teach these concepts in our online community has resulted in over 1,000 documented success stories with more popping in constantly. Dozens of these "Amazon Replens" success stories from around the world are amazing business builders who have been interviewed on my podcast at SilentJim.com.

Some of my favorite success stories are from people with no prior business experience, or teens who sign up to sell on Amazon using their parents' permission, or students with health issues that have few other income opportunities, or homeschool families who are building the business together, or professionals who have lost their career for some reason, or students who have "tried it all and failed so many times". What do these stories and so many more have in common? These are just a few of the real stories from among our students that we've interviewed - they are real people in our community of successful sellers who are using the Amazon Replens model to build six, seven and even eight figure businesses on Amazon.

Will these ideas work for you? If you are ready to learn and do the work as others have done, there's no reason this won't work. The future looks very bright for Amazon Replens sellers from our vantage point. It's just getting started!

God bless you, business building warrior! We are rooting for you and we are here for you!

Jim Cockrum
SilentJim.com
Podcaster & E-commerce Author

Part 1
–
Introduction and Mindset

Introduction

–

My Journey Will Shortcut Yours

This book is for resellers, also called third-party sellers.

Resellers look for items to buy that are inexpensive enough to sell for a profit. Of course, that describes about any business or investment. After all, Target does the same thing; Target buys things at wholesale to resell them to the public at marked-up retail prices. Stock investors look for undervalued stocks they can buy, hold, and sell for more later.

What separates third-party sellers from other businesses is that we don't generally open a physical storefront or create our own website to sell things. Instead, we like to use existing websites to sell things, such as Amazon, Walmart, eBay, Mercari, and Poshmark.

This book teaches you how to build an Amazon reselling business based on a specific strategy we call *replens.* The replens strategy can work on most reselling platforms such as eBay. Even so, we find Amazon to be the most effective reselling platform for the way we source and sell things. That's why Amazon is the platform of choice in this book.

> **Note:** I won't fully define replens for a few more pages. For now, think of replens as things you sell over and over; as they run out of stock, you *replen*ish your inventory and they sell again.

Our Story

I hope you're encouraged when you see where my family started and learn the steps we took to get to where we are now. I'm convinced you can have the same or even far greater success. This is why I want to relate how we grew our small reselling side business into a full-time active business with employees and an inventory that ranges from 750 to 1,000+ active items at any one time.

Our growth from zero to sales of $100,000 each month took about two years. That's more than a million dollars a year in sales in 24 months.

To achieve that growth, we spent the majority of our efforts doing *exactly* what you'll learn in this book. Here, you will master the step-by-step method we used. You'll be able to mirror our success and even exceed it if that's your desire, as many of our students have done.

My wife Brittany and I have been together for more than a decade. We met in high school; she was 16 and I was 17. We married young and grew into adulthood together.

While we both had separate jobs, we decided that when we have children we wanted to be set up in our own business so we could both raise them, be home together, and work together as a family growing a business. This is far easier today than it was before about 2005 thanks to technology's impact on the world.

> **Note:** We got married to be together, not to be apart. One of the primary benefits families find in reselling is that the fathers can come back home and work the business with the family.

Originally, eBay helped pave the way for people to go to their computers and later their phones, buy things they wanted, and sell things they no longer needed. About the same time eBay took off, Amazon became known as the Internet's bookstore. Amazon quickly became the largest retailer of books in the world. It only took a few years for Amazon to expand their product mix from just books to everything.

These kinds of online businesses made it possible for individuals like us to become suppliers of merchandise that Amazon and other sites sell. The massive growth of third-party reselling today is the direct result of these websites making it possible for us to participate in their supply chain.

We Went Full-Time

To boost our income after getting married, we tried our hand at reselling on Amazon. We enjoyed it enough to try to find a way to make Amazon be a central part of our family business.

The course we used to get started was the Proven Amazon Course (you can find out more at askjimmysmith.com/sell-on-amazon) and it is consistently still the best course in the market to learn online selling that is constantly updated with new courses for no additional cost! It actually has been updated to include the course this book was based on (which can be found at the same link if you are interested in just this course).

We spent about a year and a half trying to grow our Amazon business while I sold insurance in a traditional job. After that year and a half or so, it was obvious that Amazon had plenty of potential to be our full-time family business. I quit selling commercial insurance and we've focused on Amazon reselling ever since.

> **Note:** Why Amazon? It allows us the freedom to really do whatever we want in our lives. Amazon can be hard work, but it allowed us to systemize and scale our business.

Our Numbers

I never hesitate to show our Amazon growth statistics to anyone to encourage them to go do the same. Amazon is a massive selling platform. Online sales continue increasing every year, and with that increase, Amazon's services and product offerings grow. Amazon is the largest retail store on earth which is an extremely good reason to be a part of it when you resell.

The next few sections follow the timeline of events that took us from $0 in sales on Amazon to over $100,000 a month.

In the Beginning:

We began Amazon reselling in December of 2015.

June 2017:

By June of 2017, our sales grew to $8,587 per month. During this first year and a half, we were still part-time resellers. We got our inventory from store clearance aisles, deal shopping, and running around constantly looking for merchandise we could flip for a profit.

This reselling model of seeking out clearance and discounted items to source was fun for us, but it's a hustle. Finding inventory this way keeps things from being an easily sustainable reselling model. We can't consistently control when profitable sales occur. Deals come and go. With the typical model most Amazon sellers use, they can't determine which items will be sold at low enough prices to repeat the same sales month after month.

Therefore, unlike the replens strategy you'll learn in this book, when you stop looking for things to resell using the clearance model, your inventory literally drops to zero quickly. This is because you have no products to fall back on that you sell over and over. To maintain a constant inventory with the model we started with, you must constantly find things to buy that are discounted enough to sell them for a profit on Amazon.

July 2017:

The month after we topped $8,500 in sales, we joined the *Business Building Legends* reselling community. Legends is responsible for showing us what is possible not only with replens but also to instill stability in our business. I can't recommend highly enough the training and camaraderie that Legends provides its members. (You can learn about Business Building Legends and get a $1, 30-day trial here: bit.ly/legendstrial).

One month after joining Legends, in August of 2017, our sales grew to $14,190 but those sales included zero replens. I attribute the growth success we had after that month to joining Legends and learning the importance of replens.

From adding replens to our inventory mix and quickly moving exclusively to replens, in October of 2017 our sales grew to $25,223. That Q4 (fourth quarter, the three months where Amazon sales can outsell any other quarter by a factor of three or more) was great, but our growth didn't continue for the next few months as I'll explain next.

February 2018:

I quit my insurance position and we both went full-time into Amazon reselling with the goal of focusing on replenishable items almost exclusively.

March of 2018

In March, our sales dropped back to $19,327 so we'd stopped growing. We know exactly why our sales didn't continue to grow and that's because our sales *could not* continue to grow with just Brittany and me working the business.

Until we outsourced some of the operation (primarily hiring one or more assistants to help purchase, prep, and ship our items to Amazon), the two of us could only handle so much. Two people's time is limited to 48 hours total in a day. The $20,000+ monthly sales level required help in order to scale up our business to the next level it could go to.

> **Note:** Part of the material in this book addresses outsourcing parts of your business. You'll learn the benefits and things to watch out for when you hire help for your reselling business.

May 2018:

Our sales started rising again, but not by much. They reached $21,743 for the month. This was three months after I quit my job to work with Brittany full-time in our reselling business.

Our slow growth was disheartening. We both worked the business full-time, but sales didn't dramatically increase in our first three full-time months. We realized we *definitely* needed to outsource parts of our business. We had to get help if we were to continue to grow.

> **Note:** We actually were in our own way, slowing ourselves down. By trying to do it all, we began to do nothing as well as it could be done at the sales levels we wanted.

July 2018:

We hired two employees and rented warehouse space.

You certainly don't need to begin with two employees and a warehouse as early as we did. Even at our sales level, in a way getting both assistants and the warehouse was a small leap of faith because the business made it difficult to handle the new expenses and pay ourselves. Yet, we were convinced that our growth had been level only because we were trying to do it all ourselves in the confines of our home.

> **Note:** Our hired assistants primarily prepped and shipped the inventory that Brittany and I would source (buy). Freeing us up from the prep and ship process allowed us to find more replens and higher profit replens. We could also better concentrate on the business side of things such as the restocking inventory, handling returns, and dealing with Amazon requests that come from time to time in this business.

That month of July, with our warehouse and two assistants, our sales skyrocketed up to $39,124, basically double what our sales had been in almost every month prior.

August 2018:

The following month, we came close to doubling sales once again by hitting $74,175.

It's critical you understand what was in play here. We freed ourselves up to locate more replens, more inventory to sell, when we stopped having to take time out of our day to do the more routine job of preparing and shipping products to Amazon. You must understand how *quickly* a reselling business can scale up.

Reselling businesses do often begin slowly. Using the replens model you learn here, you can grow your inventory far faster, speeding up your profits, when you outsource more common tasks of your business. It's my hope that you grow faster than we did because you're going to understand how to avoid several pitfalls we didn't know how to avoid until after they caused us problems along the way.

Skipping over Q4:

Q4 sales figures are highly skewed compared to the other three quarters. Even though we broke above $100,000 two of the three months in Q4, those are inflated for the season and don't show a true growth picture that we can attribute to the replens business in general.

Therefore, I'll skip Q4 and move to the following year, 2019.

March 2019:

Sales reached $92,932 after we hired two part time shoppers and another assistant to help with some additional business.

April 2019:

Sales hit $103,700.

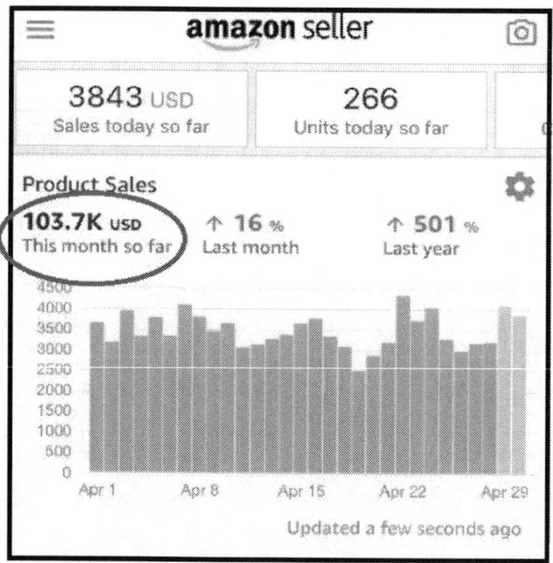

One and a Half Years

By following this timeline, you'll see it took us one and a half years to grow our sales from about $8,000 per month to over $100,000. Actually, our sales went from *$0* to $100,000 because that first month had no replens and our sales now consist almost exclusively of replens.

Additionally, the profit we were making on our sales numbers before we had employees was over 30% and now with our employees, rent, utilities, etc. we hover around 15%. Many people ask us, so I wanted to address that here.

Today, we rarely source sales and clearance the way we did when we started. The replens business offers dramatically more growth potential, consistency, and scalability than hunting discounted items to sell month after month.

April 2019 to Today

As of the time of this writing, we've consistently stayed above $100,000 per month in sales. We've continued to grow and scale our business to the point of being much more hands off. We hit our highest sales month in May of 2020 with over $190,000 in sales! We've also added in many more revenue streams to our businesses in addition to our Amazon business. This model is truly a way to get freedom to pursue the things you want to do and achieve financial freedom in the process. Scaling the replens model as I outline in this book allows you to control your business and not have your business control you. The opportunity has continued to grow and shows no signs of slowing down!

This Book's Structure

Following our timeline was critical for you to see. It's my goal that you follow our growth pattern. I'll teach you how to achieve the same growth we did with replens. Hopefully, this means I can warn you about missteps that slowed us some and I can encourage you to take a few steps faster than we took them.

I want you to have maximum success with the least number of problems along the way.

Given that, here is the general breakdown of how you'll train using this book:

Overview of Replens

In the first chapter, I'll give you a formal introduction to replens and reselling using the replens model. You'll better understand where you're headed, and you'll learn some of the nuances of this strategy.

Next, we find that it's most helpful to grow a replens business in tiers we call stages. At each stage, you move up to a new range of monthly sales. We developed these ranges based on the expected amount of work and capital required to succeed at each stage.

Here are the stages you will follow:

Stage One: $0 to $10,000

You must start somewhere. Just as it was for our business, you're beginning with zero replens. (If you happened to find one or more replens already, congratulations! Hopefully, you will be able to leverage this book's strategies to find them much faster going forth.)

This is your primary learning stage. In Stage One, you'll learn about tools that help you find replens and strategies to find your first set of replens.

> **Note:** At each stage, your goal should be to focus on getting to that stage's high sales range, in this case $10,000. You then can jump to the next stage and implement additions to the process that moves your business forward.

Your initial goal will be to find 30 replens in 30 days. You might make it a goal to find one a day or two every 15 days or whatever works for you. I'll devote more time to explaining how you can accomplish finding 30 replens in 30 days a little later.

People often ask us how much capital they need to reach $10,000 in replen sales in three months. We'll discuss capital requirements throughout the book, but for now, an initial capital of $500 to $1,000 is best, but I've seen many people start with as little as $100. The real answer depends on how well you can find initial replens.

All dollar amounts and returns discussed here assume you're building your business solely on the income generated. You only need to put new capital into the business when you initially buy your first set of replens to send into FBA.

If you need to take some capital out of your growing replens business for living expenses, this will greatly slow down the growth of your replens business. Along the same lines, if you initially need to invest less than $500, say just $300 for inventory, you'll take longer to accomplish Stage One's $10,000 monthly sales goal. But if you can reinvest your income, you *will* reach the goal much faster than if you take some out.

Stage Two: $10,000 to $40,000

Stage Two cements all your learning from Stage One. You hustle to find far more replens than you did in Stage One. You'll begin to document aspects of your business with the idea of creating training materials for people you hire in the future. Lastly, you begin to add in more software to free up your time to focus on growing your business in other ways.

Stage Three: $40,000 to $70,000

When you reach Stage Three's monthly sales levels, lots of possibilities begin to show themselves. You'll want help and fortunately you'll easily afford help. You'll seek to move your business out of your home if it's been there to this point.

> **Note:** Don't let the thought of hiring employees or seeking warehouse space frighten you. I'll walk you through each step of the process. You'll see it's actually much easier to handle hiring and payroll than you might think if you've done it. Additionally, there are options for using Prep and Ship companies to outsource this work to that we will discuss later in the book.

With new help easing your load, you'll be transitioning nicely to the Entrepreneur Mindset. All sorts of possibilities will begin to open. Your growth has the opportunity to take off far faster than ever before in this process.

Stage Four: $70,000 to $100,000

There's little to keep you from reaching $100,000 in two years or less. At sales of $1.2 million dollars a year, you'll have a new problem: too much cash!

You'll transition from thinking like a business owner to thinking like a full-time business investing entrepreneur. You'll manage your business's resources rather than work your business's resources.

Stage Five: $100,000 and Beyond

Growing past a $100,000 per month business is extremely simple once you have regular sales to fund your growth. I'll show you ways to take your incoming capital and funnel it to different kinds of business opportunities. They'll relate to your Amazon replens business but add new streams of income.

Starting Point

I assume many reading this book already have sold or sell on Amazon. This isn't a how-to-sell-on-Amazon book, it's a how-to-sell-on-Amazon-using-the-replens-strategy book. Even if you're a veteran Amazon reseller, you can benefit from just about every aspect of this book if you haven't sourced replens much before.

Hang on tight, you're about to go on a rewarding journey!

Chapter 1

–

Never Underestimate the Potential of Continuous Small Profits

In general, the easier and less risky an income stream is, the smaller it will be compared to riskier and more difficult incomes. For example, in the stock market, *risk adverse* investors (the ones uncomfortable with taking large risks) often make smaller gains than investors who tolerate more risk. Even if they make less money than their riskier friends, the risk adverse investors might sleep better at night. They know they'll lose less if investments turn against them.

As you know, this book is for those who buy items to resell on Amazon. The principles also apply to Walmart, eBay, Mercari, Facebook Marketplace, Poshmark, and other selling outlets too but the focus remains on Amazon. Still, as you grow your Amazon business, keep in mind that you can expand the concepts here to the other selling platforms.

Do you want a fast nickel or a slow dime?

Like stock market investors, different Amazon resellers tolerate different ranges of risk. Some resellers pick "low-hanging fruit" by finding lots of items to sell that make small profits. They look for fast-selling items (the "fast nickels") but many other sellers sell them too.

Due to the competitive nature of low-ranking Amazon products, these sellers might compete with 45 or more other sellers for the same items. This is okay because the items will sell even if the profit is small. Perhaps they only make 15 to 20% ROI (*Return on Investment*) but they prefer this over shipping costlier, larger, or slower-selling items into Amazon.

Others refuse to source and sell anything that doesn't return 100% ROI. (You'll learn how to calculate and use ROI later.)

In many ways, this book's strategies please risk adverse Amazon sellers who prefer to take numerous smaller profits over investing in slower-selling, higher profit items (the "slow dimes"). There's a nice plot twist here to the usual way of sourcing faster-selling items. Ultimately, you're going to learn how to find, source, and sell specific smaller profit items that sell *over and over and over*. Unlike the way many source products with clearance and store sales, once you find a replen you don't sell it once and it's done. You keep buying it over and over. You send it to Amazon to sell over and over. One by one, with new ones added to existing ones, you grow an inventory of items that sell repeatedly.

In our business, we sell over 8,000 units each month. That's how we gross $100,000+/month. We don't make that $100k selling items that each make $100 profit. Our success comes from us selling thousands of items making as little as $3 to $4 each (with a few larger profit items tossed in the mix).

Can you do the same? Can you find thousands of items each and every month that each make a few dollars in profit? Yes, you can. We began at zero items and grew from there. You can too. Is competition higher now? Perhaps, but you have a major *key* to your success that we didn't have; you have step-by-step instructions and tools in this book.

I'll tell you what failed for us and what worked for us. I'll tell you what still works for us and what will work for you. Convert any scarcity mindset you might have to an abundance mindset. That conversion is not some pie-in-the-sky motivational thing, it's a reality. Millions and millions of products compete for millions and millions of buyers every hour. There's plenty of room for you. At the time of this writing, we've had over 1,000 documented success stories (and growing!) voluntarily posted from students that went through the course and this book. To check out over 500 of them, head over to askjimmysmith.com/success.

> **Note:** If you're an Amazon reseller who doesn't mind risk and wants higher returns, you'll benefit from this book's strategies as much – perhaps *even more* – than resellers who don't prefer slower-moving, higher-profit items. This is because the goal of this book is to put the *consistent*, lower-profit items you find on autopilot. Each month, you'll buy those items without too much thought, freeing you up to focus on the higher-ROI products you like best. Even better, you can hire shoppers to buy your repeated items each month completely freeing you to focus on higher ROI products to sell. You've got the best of both worlds: a consistent, *growing* fixed income stream from repeatable products combined with a higher-returning income stream from your riskier-but-higher-profit inventory you find. You're earning *both* fast nickels and slow dimes!

Repeated Profits from Replenishables

In the selling community, you've seen that we call products that we sell month after month *replenishables* or *replens*.

The first step in you mastering the profitable world of replens is to know exactly what they are. You might think of napkins, air filters, condiments, tissues, toothpaste, bread, and detergent as examples of replens because people replenish the stock of those regularly.

A replen for the Amazon seller differs from those traditional household replenishable items.

Going forth:

- A replen is not necessarily an item the same people buy over and over. It might be, it might not be.
- A replen is an item that you *sell* over and over.

The difference is a selling perspective versus a buyer perspective.

Let's say you find a source for a half dozen 1965 Mustang replacement steering wheels each month. And each month you sell all six. After 30 days, the supplier lets you buy another six and you sell those six on Amazon.

1965 Mustang owners all over the world aren't buying replacement steering wheels each month! But obviously, every month a certain number of restorers need such a steering wheel and the demand is consistent enough for you to sell your six every month for a steady profit.

You care only about the seller's perspective here because *you're* the seller!

Our goal is locating as many items we can that sell a small number (or large number) monthly that we can restock and resell and restock and resell. The same buyer might *never* buy a second one from us, but enough consistent buyers appear to keep our inventory going out the door regularly.

Once you find a replen, what's the next step? Find another. *Rinse and repeat* as they say.

If it takes you three days to find your first replen (you'll almost certainly find it faster), then the next day you'll start your hunt for the next one. In reality, you have the ability to find a replen the first time you try and that's the goal for you. As you get more experience, finding over 20 in 1 hour will become more and more common as well.

This book is your roadmap. I know what it took for us to hit $100,000+ in sales every month. It'll be somewhat simpler for you with this book as your guide. You'll see tips to make things easier and pitfalls to avoid.

The bottom line is that replens add consistency to a reselling business. Consistency enables you to plan expenses and cash flow. Consistency enables you to grow at a realistic pace. Consistency enables you to grow to a size where you begin adding one or more team members (employees, Virtual Assistants, prep center partners, etc.). When you first begin, the idea of hiring an employee might be unthinkable. Soon, it'll be not only viable but you very likely will look forward to hiring. At that point, you're making great strides toward building your 7-figure reselling business.

But what about tanking prices?

Items go in and out of favor all the time. Anyone who's sold on Amazon knows prices can *tank* (drop rapidly), mass competition can jump on an item, and Amazon itself can start selling it. (When Amazon starts selling the same thing other sellers sell, guess who Amazon most often gives the Buy Box to?)

All this means your list of replens can and will change over time. You might sell a most excellent replen for eight months and in the ninth month that replen drops in price and you stop sourcing it.

Fortunately, a large inventory of replens changes less frequently than seller inventories without replens. Your selling risk is much lower with replens than without. Your income stream has a much greater chance of growing than without replens.

You're likely starting to view replens as a seller already. As buyers we might buy tissues every month for our family. But it could be difficult as a seller to make profit on a box of tissues. You might very well find profit there, but will it be consistent? Might it only be profitable because a store had a giant, one-time sale on tissues, and you had great coupons that month?

Such a buyer replen isn't at all necessarily a seller replen. It might be, it might not be.

The bottom line is we only look at replens as sellers. What consistently sells over and over that we can make a profit on over and over? It *might* also be a buyer replen such as paper towels or Oreo cookies, but it might also be a 1965 Mustang replacement steering wheel that nobody buys twice in a lifetime.

Replens are Generally *Not* Found on Clearance Aisles or with Coupons

In order to ensure you can buy a replen item month after month in about the same quantity and at the same price, you can't first source replens in a clearance aisle or use this week's coupons for that store or item. (Sometimes, sale items can become replens for you, but that's not the norm. We'll discuss those special cases later.)

Companies move items to clearance aisles to purge that stock from the store so that new products can take that shelf space. If you write down every product on Walmart's clearance aisle this week, the odds are extremely high that you won't find most of those items anywhere in the store in a month or two.

For the same reason, if you're looking for new replens, never base the profitability of potential replens item on coupons that might be offered that week. Coupons come and go. If a lipstick set is profitable to source only after you use an active coupon, very soon that coupon will expire, and in many cases another coupon for that item might not come along for a long time.

Many resellers also take advantage of discounted gift cards. You can go to discount gift card sites to find gift cards for Target you can buy for steep discounts, such as only 89% of face value. (Here's a great discount gift card link: bit.ly/replenraise). If it's a $100 face value card, you'd only pay $89 for the card. As with inventory on clearance aisles and coupons, discount gift cards come and go. You might buy a Target gift card for 89% of face value today and then not find a Target gift card under 98% of face value next month.

This is why you always look for a replen using the item's full price, with no use of coupons, and without using discount gift cards. If you find a profitable replen this month using one or all of those discounts, you'll rarely buy it next month for the same price.

> **Tip:** Don't *locate* replens based on sales and coupons and discounted gift cards but certainly *use* all the coupons and discount gift cards you can when buying your replens. These discounts are tremendous profit boosters for any reseller. Once you find a replen at its full, regular price, gift cards and coupons become extra profit when you're able to use them to buy those replens.

An Item on Sale *Can Sometimes* Act like a Potential Replen

Occasionally, we check sale items for possible new replens to add to our inventory. As you become more familiar with replens sourcing, you may start to notice many items go on sale regularly. Perhaps Walgreens puts the same detergent on sale every three months or so. When on sale, their Tide might be a good replen candidate.

We generally restock our replens monthly. We try never to buy more than a month's worth of the next estimated Amazon sales for each item. But in this Tide's quarterly sale case, we might buy a few to send in and keep track of that replen for a few months. When Walgreen's activates its common detergent sale a couple of months later, we'll restock that replen and send it into Amazon. We call these cyclical Replens since they are only replenishable on sales cycles.

This makes the Tide a quarterly replen instead of a monthly replen. That's fine. You'll have to adjust your numbers for the slower sales.

> **Note:** Keep your general buy-and-restock cycle on a monthly schedule. Buying only a month's worth estimated sales keeps risk low because we don't overbuy and risk price tanking down the road.

Although you'll keep most of your replens on this monthly cycle, as you spot patterns in store sales, you'll make educated decisions about sourcing a few things quarterly, semi-annually, or even annually if you wish.

We also have seasonal replens where we send the same Christmas items to FBA but only two or three months yearly. We don't stock those seasonal replens the rest of the year.

Another exception to avoiding sales happens frequently at Walmart. Walmart often runs *Rollback* sales on items and keeps those reduced prices for many months. When you spot a new rollback item, if it works as a replen at that price, you'll add it to your inventory and likely get the replen three or more times before Walmart ends the rollback sale.

We call replens that are no longer profitable drop-off items. We drop them out of our inventory. When you source a replen using Walmart's Rollback pricing, that item's drop-off might come sooner than your regular replens, but even three or four months of a replen is worth sourcing.

> **Tip:** If a Rollback replen goes back up in price after a couple of months, before you remove it from your inventory, check the price at other stores. Perhaps you can buy it lower elsewhere and keep selling it. One of the best ways to do that is to check Walmart's and other online stores' sites to see if the item is priced low enough to order online and keep your replen.

More Replen Benefits

Each time you find a profitable replen, you've got one less decision next month. In a way, you locked in a fixed income for a while. Sure, the replen might drop off in a few months, but unless and until it does, you'll have a consistent seller. All you need to do is keep your growing list of what to restock each month.

How many replens is enough? Do you stop when you get a list of ten items you can buy and sell each month? Fifty? A thousand?

The number depends on how much sourcing capital you have as well as how much time you have or how many shoppers you want to hire.

The best thing about replens is that you leverage every one of them you find. You research and find it *once*. Afterwards, you never repeat the initial work. You've leveraged that first investment in time, dividing the effort it took to find that replen by the number of months or years it sells.

Contrast that to traditional, non-replenishable methods of RA (*Retail Arbitrage*) and OA (*Online Arbitrage*). One starts each month with nothing to sell, searches stores, scans barcodes, looking for profit. The amount of sales, the number of coupons, and the value of discount gift cards determine if you locate anything to sell.

What you worked so hard to find, buy, and sell last month very well won't be profitable or findable this month.

That can be a frustrating grind.

One step forward, then one step backward. Month after month. Starting from scratch once again.

Don't start from scratch each month. Start each new month of selling with a list of items you already know will sell at a profit. As with the risk adverse stock market investor, each of your replens might not make a huge profit but they make a consistent profit. Even better, they don't require scanning and searching again.

Welcome to the world of replens where you'll walk into a store with a buy list each month while your competitors start from scratch with a blank list.

Chapter 2

–

A Successful Replen Mindset

Mindset is paramount to your success or failure. I'd like to address this all-important mindset before diving into sourcing specifics.

A Correct Mindset

> "Concerning all acts of initiative and creation, there is one elementary truth – that the moment one definitely commits oneself, then Providence moves, too."
> ~Johann Wolfgang Von Goethe

If you have a chance to go sourcing with a more successful reseller than yourself, do so. If you're able to go sourcing with a new, struggling reseller, do that too. The veteran will find far more products to source of course. He or she knows more and has practiced more. The skill came only as a result of the work. The skill, however, is not the full reason for success. Actually, the skill came only because the veteran seller did something more important than build skills. In the two sellers, you'll notice a dramatic difference in attitude.

The successful reseller *expects* to find profitable items. A struggling reseller, instead, often walks into stores lamenting the small number of profitable items he's found lately. Instead of *expecting* profits, this reseller wonders *if* profits will be found today.

We all have ups and downs in our sourcing success. Good days and bad days happen to everybody. Bad sourcing days almost never happen *often* to those with an expectant, abundance mentality. Your mindset directly impacts your success in anything you do.

Which Came First?

Does the veteran reseller have a better attitude today than when he first learned how to source? Of course. Better skills help build confidence.

I suggest though that the successful seller never had much of a negative attitude. If he did, he got past it quickly and worked to increase confidence by increasing knowledge and skills.

Many resellers resell for a few months and quit. In most cases, I suggest they didn't let their attitudes grow alongside their knowledge and skills. They hung onto the worrisome attitude that they wouldn't succeed. And they didn't.

The problem with the negative reseller's mindset is that she or he can walk into the same aisle a successful mindset reseller walks into, both of whom with identical skills, and the positive seller leaves with a cartload while the negative one leaves with nothing but dejection while thinking, "There's too much competition to find profit anymore."

The successful reseller doesn't practice some "name-it/claim-it" or New Age "Law of Attraction" thinking. Those aren't what make successful resellers. What makes you a success is your positive mindset. *You expect to find replens.* You will be more in tune to finding replens. You won't give up easily. If the first aisle nets you nothing, you go to the next.

When you expect to leave a store with at least one replen, you will have the energy and desire to understand that the next aisle over might very well produce multiple replens. And *you're* the one who's going to find them.

> **Note:** I run across plenty of replens success stories from brand new resellers and veteran resellers. If it were too late to grow a $100,000 per month replen business, I wouldn't take the time to write this book and I would not waste your time expecting you to learn an outdated strategy.

Your Work Ethic

Work ensures that you devote the proper resources, especially time, to do what your business requires. A professional work ethic enables you to treat your reselling business as a business and not as a hobby. This one thing can jumpstart your attitude and prepare you to recognize what needs to be done to be a success.

Your ultimate goal should be this: Work *on* your business instead of *in* your business.

To work *on* your business, you'll continuously look for ways to outsource tasks others can do. This frees you to focus on what you do best. This means outsourcing some activities to a Virtual Assistant (*VA*) who might take over tedious aspects such as handling routine Amazon messages, dealing with reimbursements, and so on. To be able to work *on* your business also means you'll hire on-site employees to prepare and ship your inventory to the FBA warehouses and ultimately hire shoppers. If you don't want to hire people for this, you can use a prep center (you can check out prepcenternetwork.com to see a list of approved and trusted prep centers).

You won't hire employees right away in your replen business unless you're extremely well-funded ahead of time. You don't *need* to outsource right away. You must learn the replen strategy which means *doing* the replen strategy. I'll lay out everything as we go through the book.

> **Note:** All this ties to a positive work ethic and a proper approach to business. By treating yourself as a manager,

instead of a doer of tasks others can do, your time becomes more efficient and effective. You forgo hours otherwise spent prepping and shipping by letting a $12 per hour worker do those things. You then have more $100 hours to seek and buy replens. Eventually, you'll turn over the $100/hour job you did to a $12/hour shopper to seek more revenue streams that you couldn't seek before.

This book requires the outsourcing of work as you grow your replens business. Our business never could have grown to $100,000 per month had we not hired help. However, not everyone has the goal of hitting $100,000 per month, so if you want a smaller size business you may not *need* to hire anyone.

Replens Help Make Training Employees Easier than Normal

Hiring employees to take over your prep and ship duties is much easier with a replens business model than with other reselling models. Most of this month's inventory overlaps last month's inventory. The only new items your workers deal with are new replens you add each month. With a non-replens RA and OA selling model, almost every shipment to Amazon must be prepped entirely differently. Even the way a traditional reselling model ships boxes to Amazon can differ from one week to the next.

Once you hire shoppers, you'll see how the replens model makes training them easier. Most of the items your shoppers buy this month are in the same stores and the same aisles as they were last month. Only the replens added since the previous shopping trip will be brand new to the shopper.

Cashflow

From the start you need to understand how cash flow levels affect what you can do, how much you can do, and when you can grow. You'll focus on cashflow differently at each stage of your replens growth. I'll give you specific advice on what to do and how to do it.

When just starting out, you often want and need to accept a higher profit or ROI (Return on Investment) to build cash reserves. You won't find as many replens at the higher profit level; other resellers are going to be looking for those same higher-return items. Still, you need to maximize your cashflow early. You need a higher return on your money to buy more and more replens.

A lack of cashflow hampers your ability to buy new replens until current inventory sells. This is why higher returns are critical when you start. If you focused on replens that brought only small returns, your money would be tied up longer in inventory that earns less than other items would earn. This makes it more difficult to fund the new replens your growth requires.

> **Note:** The best place to be is one where you have both slow- and fast-moving items that produce various profit level returns. You'll get there. The point here is you should know that cashflow is vital to monitor.

Most of us aren't wealthy with major cash reserves just waiting to be spent on Amazon inventory. That's why we'll often modify your cashflow strategies as we move forward.

Retail Arbitrage as Opposed to Online Arbitrage

In this book, we'll discuss both RA and OA sourcing strategies for your replens. Some resellers prefer one strategy over the other. I want you to learn both to add replens to your inventory. I'll primarily focus on RA for the purposes of this book. However, OA is covered at different points throughout as well and many of the strategies easily transfer between the two.

Part 2
–
Stage One: From $0 to $10,000

Chapter 3

–

Here We Set the Stage – Stage One

Stage One is your learning stage. You'll learn about tools critical for a replen business and you'll begin to add inventory. We'll discuss both Retail Arbitrage (RA) and Online Arbitrage (OA). You'll begin to incorporate them into your own replens business.

> **Note:** Your initial primary goal is not the $10,000 in sales but to find 30 replens in 30 days for your inventory. You might be able to find one each day, say on a lunch hour, or if you have more time, you could find a couple for 15 days each month. However you do it, you *must* agree you'll find at least 30 in 30 days.

Our Averages Work Well for Your Averages

The best place to get you selling $10,000 monthly is to show you the numbers we required of ourselves when we began. Even if you're not a "math person," you need to focus on a few simple numbers. Doing so keeps you heading directly towards your first $10,000 month of sales.

Replen math is just routine data you need in your business.

Average Selling Price

For Stage One, we have found that our replens have an average selling price (*ASP*) of $15 each. The products you source should *average* a total selling price of $15. Some might sell for $10 and some for $20. This is good for us to know so that we can properly set goals.

Sales Per Month Per Item

All the replens you find in this first group should each *average* 10 sales per month. Some replens might sell 50-100 items each month (congratulations!) while others might only sell about two or three each month. You want all 30 that you find in the first 30 days to average an expected 10 sales per month on Amazon. Don't worry about this too much, it should naturally happen – again we are setting this as a guideline for setting our goals and expectations.

Your Inventory's ROI %

Your Return on Investment (ROI) target is a 70% average (since that's what our average is). Never accept an ROI of under 40% when starting out. That range is doable for your starting average. You'll often find replens that return more than 100% ROI; some will return below 70%.

> **Note:** I'm often asked how one can possibly find replens that consistently produce returns of 70% to 100% (and higher). The answer is that we often find those kinds of ROIs when we sell on bundled and multipack Amazon listings. You'll see that it's often easier to make your target ROI and profit on a 3-pack of toothpaste than a single toothpaste.

Our current business dropped its minimum ROI to 25% for fast-moving items. These are things with a high sales velocity. Eventually, I'll tell you to be more lenient on your ROI – but not now. When we first began, our minimum ROI was 40% and we tried to average 70% overall. The 70% average is a good guideline for now.

Items that return less than 40% slow down your ability to grow your replens. Even so, it's a good exercise to consider what a lower 25% ROI means. Your money is then tied up in inventory that returns lower than it would make at a 40% minimum ROI. This is obvious, but what might not be obvious is that when you first start out, your capital is much less. You can't invest a big chunk of your money on low-returning items and grow quickly enough. This is why you will hold out for at least 40% ROI while averaging 70% overall. And again, a 75% to 100% or higher ROI for many of your items will not be difficult to find. Believe me, 70% isn't as big of a challenge as it sounds, in fact I know sellers that only accept 100% ROI or higher for new replens.

Calculating ROI Percentages

Return on Investment measures the percent of profit you make when you buy and sell something in comparison to the money you put out to purchase that item (your investment).

The Amazon Seller app (discussed later) will show you all of these numbers so you can easily figure this out.

Here's the math:

ROI = Ending Profit After all Amazon Fees / Your Purchase Price

Amazon generally averages about 33% in fees for items under $18. Let's say you pay $10 for a cake pan that sells for $30. Amazon's fees are probably about $10 so you make a profit of about $10 after your purchase cost.

10 / 10 = 1, converted to a percentage (move the decimal right two places) is 100% ROI.

Here's an example that doesn't work out to such round numbers:

You pay $8 for a bottle of hairspray that sells for $20. If Amazon selling fees are about $8 for that hairspray. Then you would get $12 minus your $8 spend equaling a $4 profit. Your ROI on that purchase will be:

$4 / $8 = 50% ROI

If you pay $7 for a bathmat that sells for $16, Amazon's selling fees might be about $6, making your profit $3 after your $7 cost, so the ROI calculation is:

$3 / $7 = 42% ROI

For this bathmat, you're getting close to the bottom ROI you'll accept at this stage.

Note: You never count general business expenses such as polybags, a Replen Dashboard subscription, or rent in an item's ROI calculation. Those are business overhead expenses and not item-specific.

ROI is a great way to determine how efficient any inventory item's use of money is. A sale that results in an ROI of 100% means you double your money: You spend $7 to turn it into $14 (a $7 profit after your cost).

Analyze Both ROI and Actual Dollar Profit

As good as a 100% ROI sounds, also consider an item's average profit in conjunction with ROI. As stated earlier, Amazon's fees are about 33% of a sale (they will vary per item but for the sake of numbers we will use 33% for these examples.) If something sells for your average target price of $15, you'll likely pay Amazon $5 and Amazon sends you the remaining $10. If you spend $5 on purchasing that product, you will profit $5 and make 100% ROI.

For higher-priced items, Amazon typically keeps a smaller percentage of the selling price for fees. For low-priced items, Amazon typically takes a higher percentage (around 40%). Other factors can increase those fees, however, even on high-priced items. If an item is extremely large and heavy, Amazon's fees might be higher than 33% of the selling price. But in general, 33% is a rough estimate to work with. Amazon keeps about a third of the money they sell your goods for.

Here is why you constantly watch both ROI and dollar profit. If you make $5 on an item that costs you $100 the ROI is horrid. That is an extremely inefficient use of your money.

The opposite can occur where your ROI is huge, but your profit is too small. If you buy a 3-pack of candy for $1 and Amazon sells it for $5.00, and you profit $0.50 then you are hitting an ROI of 50% but the high ROI is sort of meaningless because the dollar profit might not be worth your time.

Even worse, another problem with low-priced items is prices never remain the same. Just because Amazon sells the candy for $5 the day you source the candy doesn't mean the price will remain at $5. It can go up or far worse, it can drop lower. You need to have enough dollar profit *and* a high enough ROI to:

1. Make sourcing, prepping, and shipping the item worth your time
2. Make your money work efficiently for you, and
3. Have enough room in your margin to be able to still make money with fluctuating prices.

The average selling price (ASP) of a $15 item implies there is enough room for a good profit margin after Amazon's fees that fluctuating prices don't cause you to lose money. An ROI percentage of about 70% and no lower than 40% helps to ensure you don't tie up a large proportion of your money inefficiently.

Some people look at profit in percentage terms as well as absolute dollar terms. Here's a chart that compares profit and ROI in percentage terms and discusses how you might analyze them together at this stage:

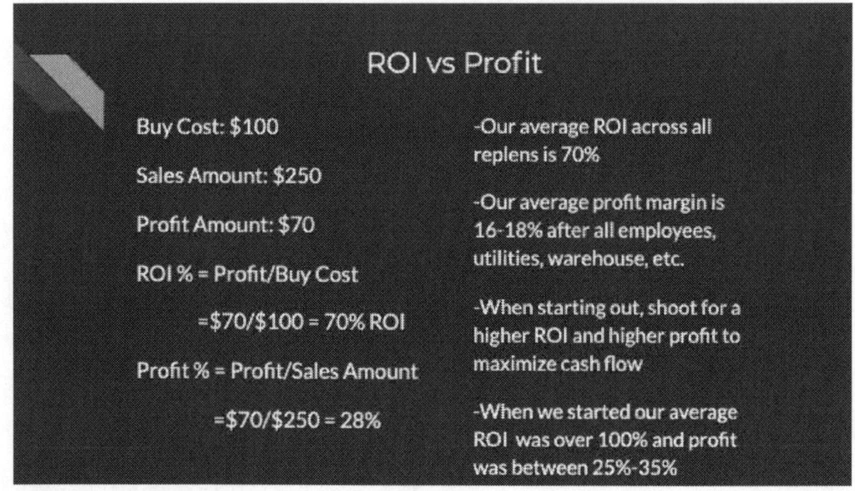

The $10,000 Math

Assuming your averages match our averages, when you reach $10,000 per month you'll be selling about 667 items. Here is how that works:

$10,000 / $15 ASP = 667 sales per month

If each replen averages 10 sales per month, you'll need 67 replens to reach the $10,000 sales goal for Stage One.

By maintaining 30 replens in 30 days, the 67 replens will take you no more than two to three months to find. In less than a quarter of the year from today, you'll be selling $10,000 on Amazon if your items match our averages.

Finding 67 replens is doable! Admit it, that's fewer than you expected isn't it? Are you beginning to realize you *can* reach $10,000 per month with replens?

Once you reach $10,000 in monthly sales, you'll be surprised at how easy you'll quadruple those for Stage Two.

Capital is the Key to Your Speed

Your beginning capital is the *only* true constraint to reaching Stage Two. $750 of upfront investment is the recommended amount to reach $10,000 in 2-3 months' time following the numbers we laid out above. If, for example, you are starting with $300 you may not reach $10,000 for four to five months depending on how successful you are at locating higher returning replens. However, even if you have $0, get creative by selling some items around your house with a garage sale, eBay, Craigslist, or Facebook Marketplace to build up some capital to start your replens business.

> **Tip:** If you have a little more patience when sourcing, you'll find higher ROIs and higher selling priced items than Stage One requires. Thus, you'll grow capital faster and stay on track to reach Stage Two faster. Don't fret if that seems too challenging. Keep in mind that even if it takes you a little longer to reach $10,000, it doesn't matter after that. At $10,000, your business has all the capital it needs to get you to the next stage and stay on schedule.

If you take it slower due to startup capital constraints, it's fine. As Amazon sells your inventory and drops the income into your account, continue patiently reinvesting those profits into funding the new replens you find.

Most importantly, just because you may not be able to *purchase* replens as fast as others, this doesn't keep you from *finding* replens every day that you can. Keep locating new replens even when your early capital is tied up in unsold inventory. Keep track of them so you don't forget about them so that when Amazon sells your current inventory, you can go to your buy list and get however many replens you previously found that you can afford.

Try to Fail Fast

Due to supply and demand, we'll never find a replen that lasts forever. Many last for months, some for years, and some won't be viable by the second month.

Amazon prices can drop. The prices you pay can and probably will rise over time. A profitable item today might not be profitable tomorrow. We call these *drop-offs*.

Your goal is to fail fast. That is, source the replens, send them in, see how they do, adjust if some fail, and move on. A positive mindset sees the single month's purchase as the cost of tuition. Each replen you find teaches you something about finding the next one. Never fall in love with a product and start hoping it comes back to profitability when the price tanks. If the price drops, study the item's history and unemotionally decide if you want to hang on a while or lower the price and break-even or take a small loss. You're not sourcing hundreds of each item and losing big money; you're only averaging 10 per replen each month. And when you first find a replen you will be testing 2-6 so that you are more protected across your whole inventory.

The 80-10-10 Rule

When doing our in-person replen trainings, at provenreplentraining.com, I like to review the 80-10-10 rule. For us, we find that 80% of the time we're purchasing correctly, we profit well. 10% of the time we break even. 10% of the time we lose a little bit of money. Those are *amazing* odds!

If you told anyone in real estate or stocks those were their odds, they'd put everything into that. For some reason, people over-analyze products and never start them. Don't over-analyze. Just start and buy replens that meet your criteria (which we will go over more later in the book).

In my private Facebook Group for Replen Sellers (which you can find at provenamazoncourse.com/replens), I made a post that highlights the power of this strategy even more. Here is what I posted (with some added explanation for the purpose of this book):

"Taking 200 ASINs (replens) for an Example

Let's say 50% of the ASINs you make 50% ROI on them (which if you're reading Keepa properly that's a LOW percentage on success and on ROI since we AVERAGE 70% ROI across 100k units per year that includes the ones we lose money on). 100 ASINs at an average cost of $5 you buy 4 a piece, so that costs you $2,000 and you profit $1,000 (again, very low ROI average of 50%).

The next 20% of the ASINs you now make 10% ROI since they were bad buys and the prices dropped. 40 ASINs at $5 a piece in cost and you bought 4 of each ASIN, that costs you $800 ($40x5x4) and you profit $80 total (10% ROI).

The next 10% you break even. 20 ASINs at $5 a piece and you bought 4 of each ASIN, that costs you $400 and you profited $0.

The last 20% you lose an average of 10% on those. 40 ASINs at $5 a piece and you bought 4 of each ASIN, that costs you $800 and you LOSE $80.

Total Spend - $4,000

Total Profit - $1,000

ROI Across the board - 25%

I was being VERY generous here in how poor these ASINs are. Typically in our business, we spend $4,000 and we MAKE $2,800 profit at that average 70% ROI.

Usually I find it's 80% you make money, 10% you break even, and the last 10% you lose money."

This just illustrates that even if you are WAY below our average ROI% and our average success rate, you STILL have an excellent business model you can pursue. Use this example as something to encourage you when things aren't going perfectly. Even at that low 25% ROI, it's way better than most investment opportunities.

Replen Erosion is a Good Thing

Don't get discouraged that you could find 75 replens the first couple of months and 10 or 15 of them stop working by the third month. Although that's a little more than we'd expect, drop-offs come and go in varying amounts. Drop-offs are the nature of this business. It might surprise you to learn that drop-offs are good!

If markets never changed, you'd not find opportunities as easily as you can now. New products appear on store shelves all the time. It's your job to get the profitable ones selling on Amazon. Replens come and go. After your first month or two, you might already replace replens here and there instead of always increasing your inventory count. Expect this.

But also understand this constant ebb and flow is the very thing that makes a lucrative replens business possible. Old opportunities die off, but new ones wait for you. If this weren't the case, the first 20 sellers who scour Kroger's for replens would eventually find them all, corner the market, and there'd be no room for any new sellers to source at Kroger's.

The nice reality is that Kroger's prices and products constantly change, Amazon's prices and products constantly change, resellers come and go, profit requirements change, capital available to buy inventory changes, and all these changes are what makes it possible for you, a brand new replen reseller, to walk into any Kroger's and find plenty of replens with rare exception.

Chapter 4
–
Your Replens Toolbox

Mastering certain tools early in your replens journey makes success possible. If you've sold items on Amazon before, as most of you probably have, you're already familiar with many of the tools you need. You might even be an expert.

Even if you know the tools I'm about to describe, you'll learn how to apply them to build a successful replens business. You then won't have to learn them from scratch, and the replens-related concepts will sink in fast.

The Essentials

All resellers end up with a set of sourcing tools that suit them best. A few tools are essential to everybody who does RA and OA.

A Seller App

The one tool you require (assuming you have a smart phone, either Android or Apple) is a seller app. If you're an Amazon seller, you have full access to the most common seller app already and that's the Amazon Seller App pictured next.

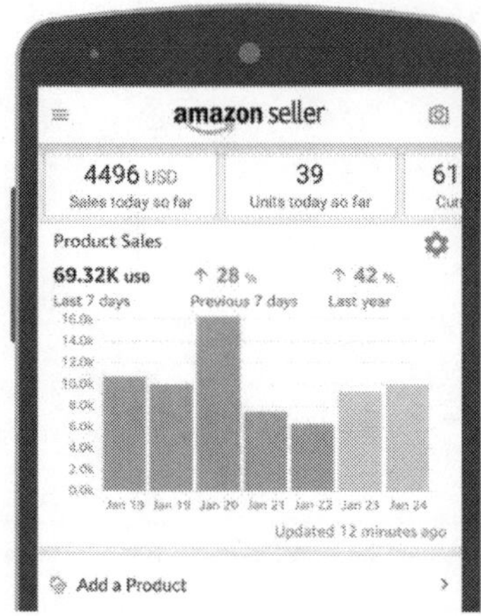

Other seller apps are available, some for a monthly subscription fee and some are part of another subscription you might already have.

If you subscribe to InventoryLab for Amazon accounting and shipping management, you have free access to the Scoutify scanning app. Scoutify offers more features than the Amazon seller app such as creating Buy Lists, access to Keepa, and some other data points.

> **Note:** I have my favorite recommended sourcing app constantly updated at my website at askjimmysmith.com/best-resources – Scoutify is great for creating buy lists, but there are better apps out there to help you find more products as Scoutify does have limitations from a sourcing perspective.

Even pros who primarily use another sourcing app such as Scoutify still check their Amazon Seller app when sourcing. The Amazon Seller app doesn't always provide the most efficient and effective sourcing tools but other data available within the app comes in handy. That's why when seeking replens, you'll often have both the Amazon Seller app and a secondary app such as Scoutify app open, going back and forth to verify information.

> **Note:** If one seller app did everything you'll ever need, you'd only need that one. No seller app does everything.

> Until the day comes where one tool does it all, we'll be switching between Amazon's seller app and whatever other app we routinely use.

Keepa

In addition to at least one seller app, you need Keepa access. Keepa helps you find profitable items that might not look profitable at first. Keepa also serves as a warning against bad buys that can falsely otherwise look good.

Keepa works in conjunction with your seller app. You need both tools to make the best sourcing decisions. Both are available for your phone. When sourcing in a store, you can switch from your seller app to the Keepa.com website to analyze potential replens.

Some seller apps now integrate Keepa to one degree or another. With these, you can check Keepa from within the app without leaving the seller app. Scoutify gives you access to Keepa. This keeps you from switching back and forth between a seller app and the Keepa.com website on your phone. The Amazon Seller app provides no Keepa access.

> **Note:** Keepa requires a negligible monthly subscription of about $17 at the time of this writing. If you're short on funds, $17 each month might seem like a high cost right now. You can lose far more than $17 on one or two bad buys Keepa could have warned you about. Keepa is necessary.

I'll provide some Keepa training in a bit. If you already know how to use Keepa, you'll still get extra understanding of how to use Keepa for replen decisions.

Patience and Mindset

The final must-have tools are patience and mindset.

When first starting out, some people pick up the replens concept quickly. For others, it can take a few days or weeks to get the hang of it. Patience is rewarded. Fight the temptation to get frustrated on outings where you find nothing to resell. If this business required no real effort, everybody would do it and it would immediately lose profitability!

Get comfortable being uncomfortable.

This is one of the Navy Seals' motivational phrases to improve mindset. Such a mindset prepares you to handle situations that come up, including the early days of replens when you may not locate them as well or as fast as you'd like.

In many situations like business, it's good to be uncomfortable because it means you're moving forward, growing, trying new things. Getting comfortable at being uncomfortable means you show up, day after day, week after week, and follow through to hit your $100,000 sales per month goal.

Replens with Retail Arbitrage requires many days the first several months of you standing in aisles a long time. If you choose to source using OA, you'll be searching websites a long time. Either way, it's an uncomfortable thing to remain there, slowly powering away.

Focus from the start and remind yourself you're in this to build your business. The effort will work. A lot of people start an Amazon business but stop early, they don't move forward, they fall off and move away from selling just as their skill starts to grow. They could have made a great go of it if they just pushed away the negativity a little longer.

Failure is a Piece of Data, Not a Personal Value Judgement

A *feedback loop* occurs when we tell ourselves something after an event happens. If we continue to give ourselves the same feedback and that feedback is unproductive or negative, that same failure is likely to loop right back the next time.

"I have not failed. I've just found 10,000 ways that won't work."
~ Thomas A. Edison

When you begin your search for replens and you fail the first day, two days, or three days, you might start to tell yourself things like:

- *I'm no good at this!*
- *There are no good products out there!*
- *I'm just not getting it!*
- *Prices are too high to let me reach my replen goal this month!*
- *Replens must be dead!*

You may consider yourself a failure at replens. If so, you will get the urge to drop it and try something else.

The problem with such a negative feedback loop is you're telling yourself the wrong thing. While it's true you aren't as good at finding replens as I am, *you just started, and you can eventually be as good as I am and even far better.*

Your early failures are pieces of data to analyze. In the early days of any new process, time is often the solution. You need more time hunting replens. That's why I mentioned patience before mindset in the previous section. You must be patient. You must be comfortable being uncomfortable by not finding replens right away.

Just because you might fail to find replens tomorrow doesn't mean you'll fail the day after tomorrow. It means you found none one day, *not every day*. It means you might need to review replen strategies again. It means you need to make sure you understand how to search for replens without skipping any steps.

> **Note:** Think of it this way. If a business buys billboard advertising and in the three months, business doesn't increase, in no way does that mean it's foolish to advertise on billboards. That experience only means *that billboard advertising venture* didn't work. Instead of a feedback loop of *"Billboards are a waste of advertising dollars,"* a better feedback loop might be: *"Was our billboard located in the same part of town our target customer typically drives by?"* and *"Did we say too much or too little on the billboard?"* and *"Could we hire an advertising firm to*

produce more effective billboards for our company?" and *"Are billboards the best way for our business to advertise?"*

Those are positive feedback loops that treat the failure as a piece of data. The response to failure should be analysis and not dejection. If you change the location, the message, or the offer and buy another billboard, that one might succeed. It might fail worse. Either way, you learn valuable information about what to do next. With each piece of information, you make the *next* dollar you spend on advertising a wiser dollar.

Failure is Tuition

A day or two without finding a replen is the investment you make honing replen skills, mastering patience that makes you money, and treating your business like an investment instead of a job.

Chapter 5

–

The Fundamentals: Finding Replens with RA or OA

You're ready to begin the foundation of all replens businesses: Finding the replens.

Go Slowly

If you go fast and try to speed up the process, you can easily miss a bunch of products that would work as replens. Missing a replen because you were in a hurry costs time to locate another. It also costs money in lost revenue you'll not get from items you missed.

Don't Scan UPC Barcodes

As most people who've looked for items in stores to resell know, you can often scan an item's UPC barcode in the Amazon Seller app to see that product's Amazon sales page. Sometimes multiple listings appear that include that UPC, such as a bundle. Even though your selling app might display one or more listings from a UPC scan. Many items with UPC codes sell in many different ways on Amazon but never mention the UPC. You'll never see those if you scan the UPC.

Looking for replens by scanning UPCs is faster than typing an item's name into your scanning app. Nevertheless, scanning the UPC finds *far fewer* listings. Scanning the UPC barcode on a package of *Dustbuster* hand-held vacuum filter package might produce five Amazon listings that bag sells on. One or more may be profitable but often none will be. The majority of resellers scan UPC codes to find listings. Many won't take the time to type *Dustbuster vacuum bags* but *you* will take the time. Remember I said take things slowly. Your reward will likely be *ten or more* times as many potential listings you can sell those bags on. The odds of one of those being profitable are higher than when you only get to look at 4 or 5 matches.

Many people create Amazon listings without using the item's UPC code. These listings might be different bundles of multiple Dustbuster vacuum bags. They might be multipacks which are the very thing our business prefers to source. We'd never have located the majority of our $100,000 per month replens inventory as fast if we'd scanned barcodes only.

You'll find more listings to sell on when you type the item into your seller app. Consider this: buyers find things by typing short phrases. Buyers *never scan* UPC codes to locate things to buy on Amazon.

> **Tip:** Most cell phones are set up to let you speak into the phone instead of typing with the keyboard. Use this voice-to-text feature to save time when looking for the listings to sell on.

Approach your sourcing by finding listings the way buyers find them. Ask yourself, "How would I find this item if I wanted to buy it?" Amazon does its best to respond to buyers, not to sellers. Amazon wants every buyer who looks for something to find many product combinations so that somewhere in the results awaits something each buyer will want.

Start Broad then Get Specific

When you get to the item on the shelf to search for, first search broadly then narrow down your search. That's how you locate as many potential listings to sell on that you can.

Just type the brand name and item into your seller app. If you're sourcing in a store's office supply aisle and the next item you see is a package of six blue Pilot pens, type the following into your selling app:

Pilot pens

Starting your search with just the brand name and type of product produces the most search results. Many results won't match but you'll get a far better idea of what can be profitable in that section. As you scroll through the listings, some may stand out as having a higher-than-expected price. You're in the pens section already so if you see a few high-priced pilot pens listings with a decent sales rank (we'll discuss rank as it applies to replens a little later), look around the nearby shelves. You might find what that higher-priced listing contains.

Understand that your goal is to see if the Pilot pens in front of you are worth selling. You want to find as many listings that sell those specific Pilot pens as possible. If you search *pilot pens*, many results show up that don't match the ones directly in front of you. Great! Scroll through all those listings. If any with unusually high prices appear for what seems to be sold, see if you can find that item somewhere close by. (You'll return to the specific pens you're in front of later.)

Perhaps there's a listing with Pentel pencils bundled with the Pilot pens. If you find those Pentel pencils, check prices to see if you can buy those cheaply enough to sell on that higher-priced listing. If yes, you have a replen!

> **Note:** Don't worry about uppercase. *Pilot pens, pilot pens, PILOT PENS, and pilot Pens* all produce the same results. Interestingly, different seller apps return different sets of listings from the same search. The more apps you check, the more listing variety you'll find to sell on that might be profitable.

As you look through searched listings, small differences like color can command higher prices than others. If you're in front of a pack of blue pens but the general search shows the same pens in red are higher priced, look for the red pens. You may have just found a potential replen through what we term *reverse sourcing*; you saw a profitable listing and *then* found the item to sell on that listing.

You would have reached the aisle's red pens eventually. Replen hunting requires that you analyze each and every item on an aisle. Reverse sourcing the red pens and finding that replen early simply sped up your work. You don't want to rush any process, but within each element of sourcing you'll learn faster ways to do what you're already doing. Speaking into your phone instead of typing is quicker. Reverse sourcing often finds replens faster than searching item by item.

Here's what you might get when typing *pilot pens* into the Amazon seller app:

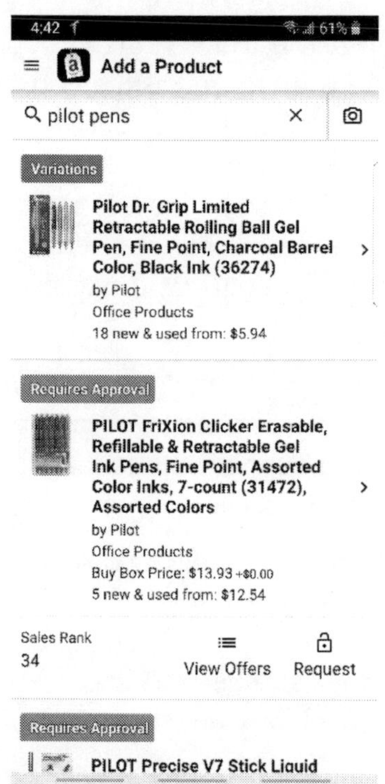

Notice the user account on this search is gated in Pilot pens and requires approval before being able to sell them. If you find yourself gated on an item, inside the Amazon seller app click the *Requested for Approval* button that pops up. You might become approved instantly. If you don't get instant auto-approval, stop looking up Pilot pens until you're allowed to sell them. There are tons of items in every store that you're not gated in, so don't worry if you see this pop up from time to time.

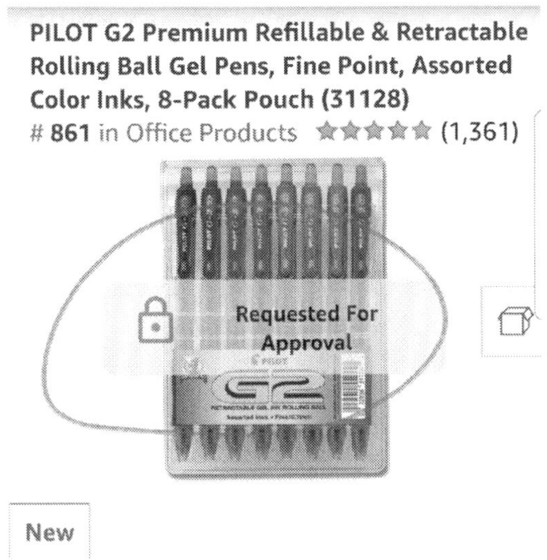

Narrowing the Results

The advantage to a general search is the large number of listings that appear. The disadvantage to a general search is the large number of listings that appear!

The many results let you spend time looking around the aisle for quick and profitable replens. Most of those listings will produce items unrelated to what you're looking for. That's the nature of general searches.

After general searching, take each product individually and check to see if it's profitable. After the overall general search, on branded products such as Pilot pens, get specific, one product at a time, by typing more specific product searches that match this pattern:

Brand Name, Type of Product, Size of Product (ounces or count), etc.

For a pack of six blue Pilot pens in front of me, I might type:

pilot pen 6 count blue

This narrows down the search, produces listings that more closely match the item I'm in front of (or looking at online when doing OA), and produces a higher quality set of listings to sell on.

As you get more specific, the listings more likely include the item you're in front of.

Don't overthink your search. If you search for too many specific words, you'll shortchange the number of listings that pop up. Remember to act like a buyer when sourcing, not like a seller.

Typing *Aim kids gel fluoride toothpaste mega bubble berry* might display 4 or 5 results. You could look through those for profitability. But a buyer wouldn't type so many words. The more specific you get, the more you limit results. Again, you'll initially want to type a general search for Aim Toothpaste. Once you look through many general results, whether you find a profitable replen or not, get specific on each Aim in front of you.

Therefore, if you're in front of 4.4-ounce tubes of Aim Kids Mega Bubble Berry Anticavity Fluoride toothpaste, a middle-of-the-road phrase might be:

Aim kids toothpaste bubble

Bundles Rule

Whether you find potential profit or not, next add words like *bundle*, *set*, *pack*, or *variety* to the search. No search returns all possible listings. Your general and then specific searches may not produce every Aim toothpaste 6-pack Amazon sells. Adding *bundle* or *pack* could result in profitable bundles. That's exactly how we find many of our bundle and multipack replens.

You'll get a feel for which bundle term works best in different departments. Until then, if you add *bundle* to your search and hardly anything appears, try *pack* and then *variety* if you still need more listings. When looking for just about any item, the odds are great it's on a bundled listing of some kind.

How Long Do You Search for Each Item?

I dislike answering any question like this, but: it depends.

You'll hone your skills rather quickly if you take your time in each aisle. By going slowly, you increase your speed in the long run. That's true of anything you're new to. If you try to shortcut the sourcing process by skipping past things you tell yourself, "that's probably not profitable," you'll hardly ever develop good sourcing skills. Worse, you'll miss replens. Go slowly. Do everything right. Eventually, you'll familiarize yourself with some product lines enough to assume some things aren't profitable and that's fine. But this only works if you have the experience to have studied those specific brands and products enough to know what sells well and what doesn't.

Try Picture Scans

One final search method to try is a *picture scan*. At the time of this writing, only the Amazon Seller app can scan visually. Even if you regularly use a more powerful scanning app, you'll use Amazon's Seller app if you want to scan an item visually.

To picture scan, you will:

1. Start the Amazon Seller app.
2. Click the words, "Add a Product," near the center of the app's screen.
3. Click the camera icon in the upper-right hand corner.
4. Center the item on your app's screen. Tiny dots of light will flicker while Amazon attempts to locate that item in its database.

> **Tip:** If nothing matches after a few seconds, cover as many of the product's letters as you can and rescan. This often works best for toys like Legos where many boxes might have similar titles in the same font. By hiding the text, you give the Seller app the opportunity to focus on the unique aspect of the item without the text confusing things.

5. Once Amazon locates what it thinks is a match, you'll see one or more listings to scroll through. Picture scans almost always produce multiple listings.

> **Note:** The picture scan technology isn't perfect by any means. One or more results might not have anything to do with the item you scanned. Sometimes, a picture scan produces a long list of "matches" but not one item in the list actually matches. Picture scanning offers an added way to produce different sets of listings you didn't find before with keyword searching.

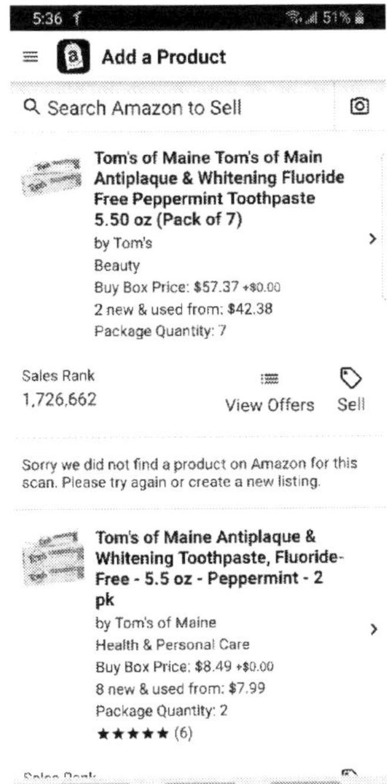

Note: Fortunately, as with anything, picture scanning takes longer to explain here than it takes to do. Once you picture scan a dozen or so items, you'll be a champ at it and you'll find good listings often faster than you did using the (failed) method of scanning barcodes.

I suggest you type your searches (or speak them) instead of picture scanning. We have more control over what gets searched for. Typing produces better candidates. Still, nobody can guess all the keywords that sellers used to create listings. That's why picture scans can be a good tool.

If, for example, you're scanning the Tom's toothpastes and can't find good results for one of them, you're probably skipping a critical keyword. Many Tom's toothpastes are fluoride-free. Some buyers are adamant about giving their family fluoride-free toothpaste due to health concerns. Therefore, *fluoride free* is an important keyword phrase but you may not know how critical that is when standing in an aisle going from item to item.

If you're hunting for several Tom's toothpastes in front of you but find only a few listings, a picture scan might produce better results than typing because you didn't know to include the vital *fluoride free* in your search.

> **Tip:** Many times, picture scan works with pictures on websites and not just with physical products. If you're doing OA and can't seem to find good listings for an item on the screen, isolate the image and picture scan it. Amazon's seller app will locate listings with that picture in them.

Keepa is a Keeper

As I mentioned earlier, Keepa is a must-have tool in your replens arsenal. Becoming a high-level expert in Keepa would take an entire book. Fortunately, you don't have to be a Keepa ninja to know all you need for successful replens hunting.

You'll quickly master needed Keepa skills in the next chapter.

Chapter 6
–
Replens and Keepa

Some of you know how to use Keepa. Great! Still, I suggest you read through this chapter anyway. I'll hit highlights that will help you find replens faster than you normally might. If you're an absolute beginner to Keepa, we'll start with an introduction to bring you up to speed.

ACK!

Travis Hettenbach, one of the Business Building Legends leaders and a good friend of mine, coined the phrase *Ack!* It's so fitting, many of us adopted it as our daily sourcing mindset.

> "Ack! – Always Check Keepa!"
> ~ Travis Hettenbach

If you source ten profitable items but don't check Keepa, the chance you end up with money-losing items is high. The chance you skipped over profitable items is high too.

Keepa protects you from bad buys and helps locate good buys. Here's the bottom-line reason why: Your Amazon Seller App gives you a picture, a snapshot in time. The Seller App is horrible at giving you long-term perspectives of any product.

If you're looking at swimming pool brushes, but the prices aren't enough to justify sourcing any of them, you move to the next aisle.

You aren't likely to waste your time on swimming pool brushes ever again.

The problem wasn't necessarily low-profit pool brushes. The problem was that you looked at them in late December with ice on the ground. If you happened to check back in four months, much of those unprofitable pool accessories might be profitable.

Extreme seasonal items such as swimming pool supplies should obviously be checked when that equipment is about to come back into demand. Other items you source, however, might be seasonal and not as obvious that they're seasonal. This is where Keepa rescues you from bad sourcing decisions. A quick look at Keepa would tell you to head straight back to the pool supply aisle in mid-March.

If, however, it's late August, much of the equipment might look profitable *but may not be profitable more than a week or two longer* since pool season is coming to an end in the majority of the country.

Your selling app works like a camera in that it shows one frame at a time, not a movie. If a slow-selling item with a terrible rank happens to sell five the night before you found it in a store, the rank will temporarily look greater than it is the other 365 days of the year. A price tanking seller could have unloaded all his inventory yesterday, skewing the rank chart so it looked great. The other sellers' prices kicked back into the Buy Box before you checked the item, so it *appears* to be a great seller.

Keepa works like an Amazon product video camera, not a picture camera. By always checking Keepa (*ACK!*), you quickly rule out or rule in items. If a rank indicates an extremely slow seller but a recent day had a bunch of out-of-the-ordinary sales, Keepa keeps you from buying it based on that anomaly.

Make these Keepa checks on *every item* you source (we will cover these in detail):

1. Does the Buy Box price hold fairly steady when looking at its history?

2. Are there regular sales on the product?
3. Does it show sellers regularly coming in and out of the listing (indicating sales for those sellers)?

You might recall Keepa can reveal products that don't look profitable that actually are over time. This means you could check every item's Keepa chart even if the Buy Box and sales rank are poor.

You may or may not always want to take the time to view a Keepa chart on items where all the prices and ranks are poor. You certainly will catch a few hidden jewels that initially look bad, but I don't check Keepa on *all* matching listings I source. After a while, you'll begin to spot unprofitable listings faster without needing to check Keepa. The important thing is to check Keepa on *all* items that *look* profitable. You're more likely to make bad buys if you don't let Keepa warn you.

I always default to checking Keepa.

The Basics of Keepa

Keepa produces three charts for everything on Amazon, but we only look at 2 of them – the top & bottom charts. The one in the middle is basically the same as the top, but for sub-categories on Amazon and doesn't factor into our buying decisions often. The charts represent sales over time. There's always more you can learn about Keepa, but the basics are simple to master. If you're new to Keepa, the following pages bring you up to speed.

Where to Find Keepa

Once you subscribe to Keepa at Keepa.com, you'll access Keepa charts from any computer or cell phone. Always sign in to get the full data set. Here's a typical Keepa screen showing the two main charts for a product on Amazon, the middle one has been removed for the purposes of this book:

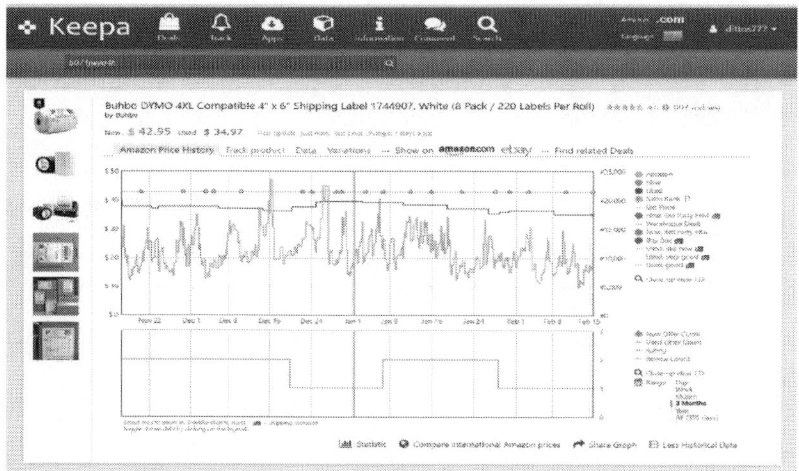

You can also access and use Keepa.com from your cell phone:

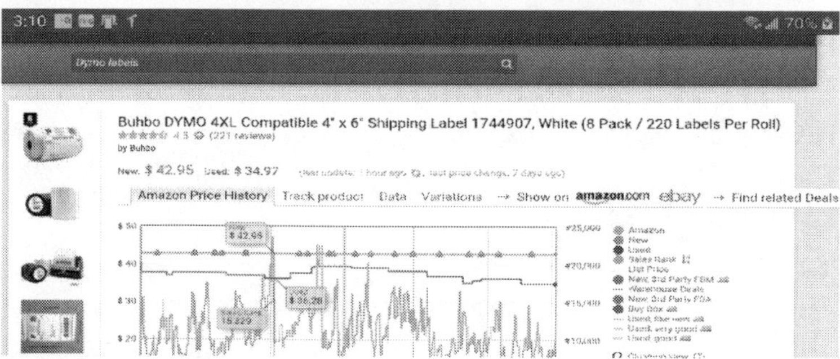

Additionally, there is a Keepa phone app, however it does not help with sourcing since it's lacking many features that us sellers need. Fortunately, some seller apps give you fast access to Keepa within the app. For example, the Scoutify app lets you jump from an item's description to the item's Keepa chart with just a click or two of buttons. This is why you often access Keepa from within a seller app and not by switching back and forth between a selling app and the cell phone's browser.

> **Note:** The Amazon seller app offers no shortcut to Keepa. If you use only the Amazon seller app, you need to switch back and forth to your phone's web browser for Keepa charts. That works until you have more funds to get a seller app that offers Keepa from the app.

When doing OA, you can open the Keepa.com page in a second window to check Keepa on a computer or laptop. Even better, if you use the computer's Chrome browser, install the Keepa extension to display a Keepa chart from directly inside any Amazon item's description page.

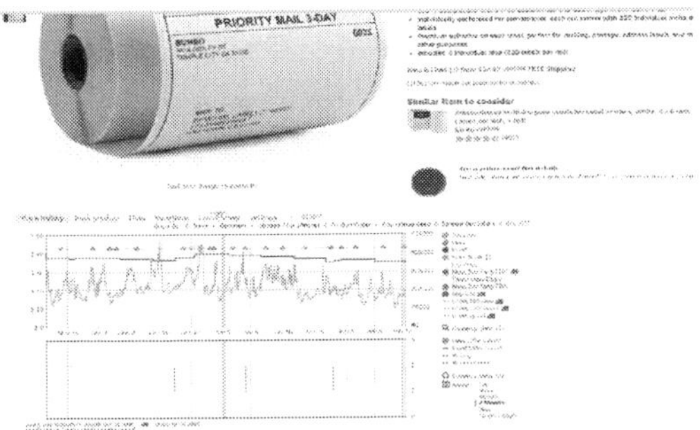

What Keepa Tells You

Keepa charts can display large amounts of sales history for any item on Amazon. (The exception is if it's a newly listed item.)

To learn about Keepa, open whatever Keepa chart is available and follow along below. Search for a popular item, like a fast-selling Lego toy, and look at the graph to find the following information:

- Sales History (the green line)
- Buy Box Price History (pink dots and pink lines)
- Amazon on the Listing (orange shaded areas)
- Seller Count History (the third box under More Historical Data shown by the purple line)
- New 3rd Party FBA Price (orange triangles)
- New MF Price (blue dots)
- The Statistics tab displays High, Low, and Average information for Price and Sales

> **Note:** If you haven't yet subscribed to Keepa, you won't be able to view all this information.

If you're reading the paperback version of this book, all charts are in black and white. You won't see the various Keepa icon colors and lines. That's okay. As stated above, each different kind of information is color-coded *and* shows in a different shape. A couple of lines, most notably the Sales Rank and Price lines, both show as black lines in the book, but their context makes them easy to distinguish.

Prepare Keepa Charts for Replens Sourcing

After subscribing to Keepa, sign in so you have full access to all the data. On the right side of a chart, you can show or hide whatever information you want. To show or hide the Sales Rank line for example, touch (on your phone) or click (on a computer) the Sales Rank option to the upper-right of the chart to show or hide the line on the graph.

The following are Keepa chart data values you'll always show when searching for replens. (If you show more than you need, the charts get cluttered and difficult to analyze, especially on cell phones. As you master advanced Keepa strategies, you'll show more data but for replens, these are fine.)

- Amazon
- New Price
- Sales Rank
- New 3rd Party FBA
- Buy Box
- New Offer Count

Amazon, if it's ever sold on the listing in the graph, shows up as an orange shaded area under the New Price line.

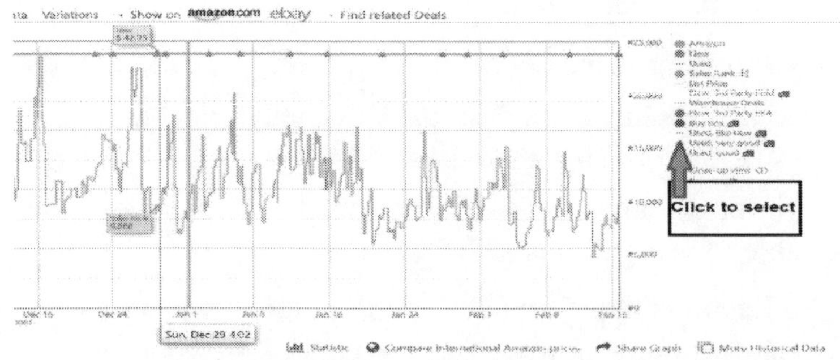

Display all charts that Keepa can show for any product. If you don't see a second or third chart below the one shown above, click *More Historical Data* in the lower-right hand corner. The top chart shows product information while the bottom chart shows seller information.

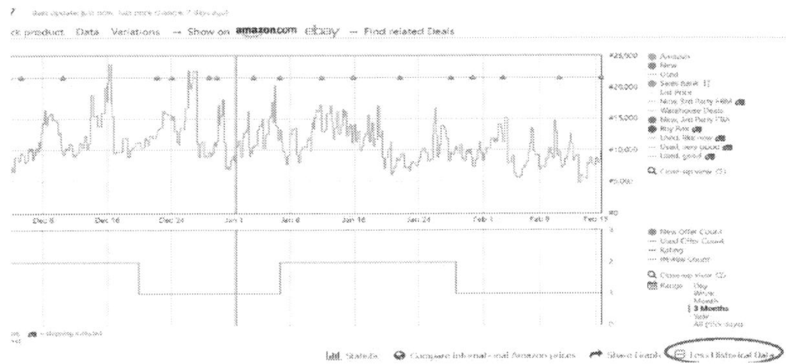

> **Note:** Once you select the display options, Keepa remembers them.

Checking Sales Rank for Approximate Sales Estimates

For those reading the paperback version of this book, the green Sales Rank line is often (not always) more volatile than the purple New Price line. Therefore, in the previous upper graph, Sales Rank is the bottom line showing far more activity than the fairly stable New Price towards the top. In most charts, the New Price line fluctuate more than this, but rarely as much as the Sales Rank.

The green Sales Rank line shows the product's historical sales rank. The more it fluctuates the better. Lots of Sales Rank movement means the item sells frequently. If a Sales Rank line shows fewer fluctuations, that generally means fewer sales (lower velocity).

Just because the Sales Rank line doesn't fluctuate a lot, won't necessarily rule out a replen. Many factors go into sourcing decisions. If relatively few drops in the green Sales Rank line appear, you can count the number of drops to see the minimum amount of sales that occurred in that time frame. Therefore, if you see 10 drops in the green line for one month's time period, the item sold at least 10 units that month. The reason it's the minimum is because a drop in sales rank could have had 2 or 3 items in 1 order or multiple orders in one close period & Keepa only captured 1 drop.

In the chart above, the Sales Rank line dips quite often, sometimes a lot and sometimes a little. On busier charts like this, you can't assume *every* small drop is a sale because noise enters busy charts. Still, even though you can't count the exact number of sales, you know that the item sells well.

> **Note:** Remember, the *lower* a Sales Rank, the better it sells. Sales rank numbers appear on the right edge of a typical Keepa chart.

In the next chart, the green Sales Rank line primarily stays under 600, an extremely low range – therefore, a great rank. For the Grocery category, it's an extremely fast-selling product. Too many drops and shifts appear in the Sales Rank line to count exactly how many sold, but you know a lot sold which is really all you need to know with that kind of rank line.

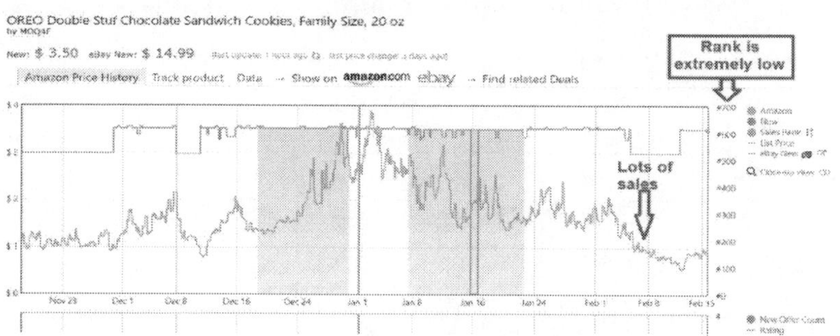

In the next graph, the green Sales Rank line shows a much higher sales rank range. Each dip in the Sales Rank line does usually represent a sale. In a slow-selling chart, count the dips within a month's time range to estimate the minimum amount of sales that occurred.

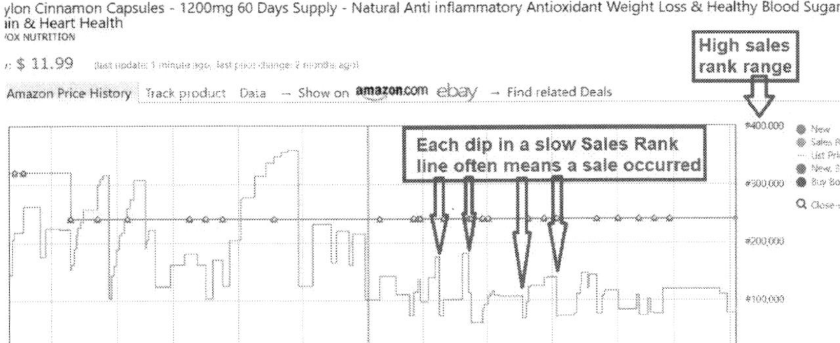

To preview things, if an item only sold seven times last month, and the rest of the Keepa chart indicates that's common, it won't necessarily mean you stay away from sourcing it if it's profitable. If you can match your selling price to the typical Buy Box price, you might be able to sell two or three each month. The only way to know is to test a few.

High sales ranks mean you test buy far fewer items to see how they do. This skews your average number of items sold down, so you need to make up for that by sourcing another item or two you expect to sell far more than ten monthly.

A general replen candidate would see at least five drops in sales rank each month before you'd test it, if you're a newer seller. Once you're experienced, you don't need to follow this rule as you may have other reasons to buy slower selling replens. Of course, the profitability must be there before you do anything with it. If unprofitable, you don't buy any to test no matter what the Sales Rank line shows.

Changing Keepa's Timeframe

By default, Keepa charts display only the most recent three months of data. To avoid getting caught up in seasonal fluctuations, *always* check the past year of sales. Every time you check a possible replen's Keepa chart, try to look at an entire year of data.

Assuming the listing isn't new, you can extend a chart's timeframe and look at the item's past year or multi-year sales history.

The following chart is a default 3-month Keepa chart:

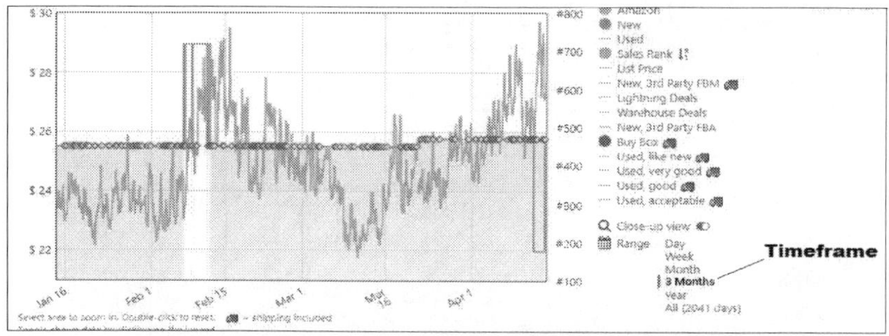

You can look at the dateline across the bottom edge of the graph to see the dates the chart represents. The Range option at the right of the chart shows that *3 Months* is selected.

If, on your phone or computer, you clicked the *Year* option below *3 Months*, Keepa would instantly give you that longer-term view of this item's history:

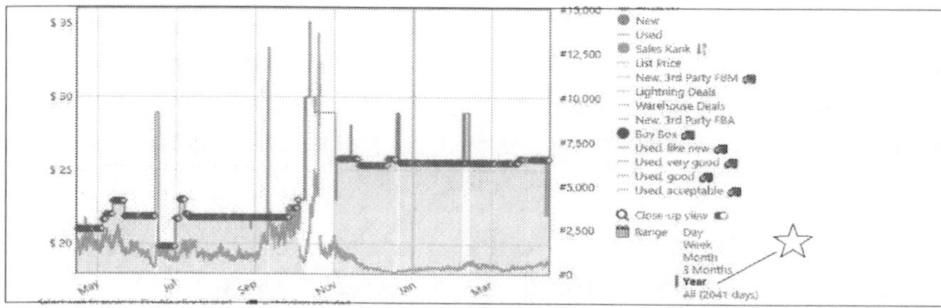

This isn't the easiest chart to look closely at. One reason that's true is because the time frame is a full year and not just three months. The item sells well with a relatively low sales rank, so the green Sales Rank line moves up and down quickly. This is the *same product* as the one in the previous graph but with a wider historical perspective. (The purple New Price line is mostly hidden by the row of pink Buy Box circles.)

> **Note:** The orange shaded areas show when Amazon sold the product along with the third-party sellers.

In this graph, we see Amazon ran out of inventory at least four times in the past year. (The third time might be difficult to see, but Amazon's shading shows a thin white break at the end of

December.) Amazon's been on this listing far more often than it's not been.

You can often tell from a year or greater timeframe that Amazon might jump on listings at only certain times of the year. For example, Amazon might sell green party hats around St. Patrick's Day but never other times. If you looked at a 3-month Keepa graph a month before the St. Patrick's Day, you might wrongly think Amazon owns the sales and never lets go. But if you expand that graph to a year, you'll see Amazon's only on the listing three months leading up to the holiday.

The rest of the year, those same green party hats might sell well but with Amazon absent. Such a listing might be a seasonal replen opportunity for you. But instead of selling *in season*, you might want to skip the season Amazon's on the product and resume selling that item the rest of the year.

It's interesting to look at the previous one-year Keepa chart at the four times Amazon did run out of stock. The New Price line dramatically spiked with sellers taking advantage of Amazon no longer holding the price down. The Buy Box didn't change much during these times, but I can tell you from the Offer count (discussed next) that the number of sellers dropped considerably without Amazon. Many sellers on this listing sold out during Amazon's absence. Sellers often priced higher than the Buy Box price but still got the sale.

Here's the same graph showing five and a half years of Keepa data:

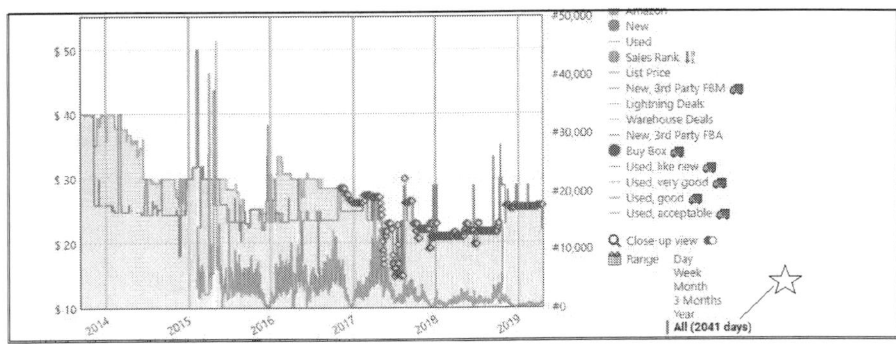

> **Note:** The **All** count under the **Range** to the right of the graph shows how many days of pricing data Keepa can display. In this example, Keepa can show up to 2,041 days of history which is about 5.5 years.

Now *that's* a busy chart.

The data is so squeezed, you can't glean a lot of sourcing information from such a long-term chart. You can see the historical price from the beginning ($40). You can see that the price dropped about $10 over its history, then bounced up, but never got close to its original price.

Rarely will you need this long of timeframe. A year or two-year chart verify if trends are anomalies or seasonal fluctuations you can expect going forth. Perhaps an item looks like a big seller during the Christmas season. You can display two years of data to see if that has been true the past two Christmas holidays.

You can see that Keepa only gives you these six time options to select from:

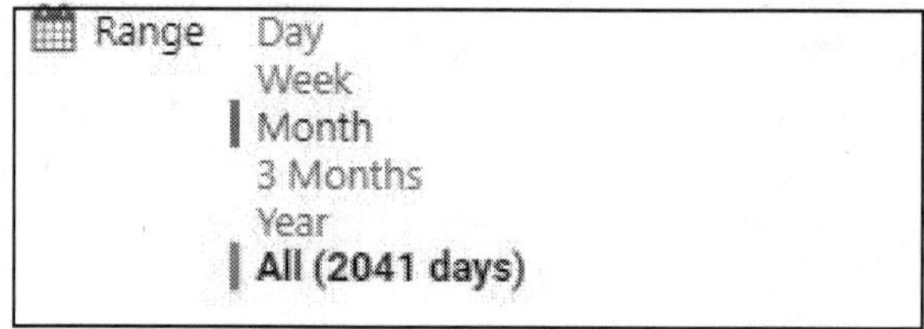

When you want a different time period, such as two years, use your mouse if on a laptop or desktop, or your pinched fingers if on a phone or tablet, to zoom in to the timeframe *you* want to see.

With your mouse on a laptop, for example, you can change this 5.5-year chart to any shorter timeframe. Point your mouse cursor to the right edge of the graph, click and hold your mouse button down, and drag your mouse to the left. This highlights the portion of the graph you're selecting as shown below:

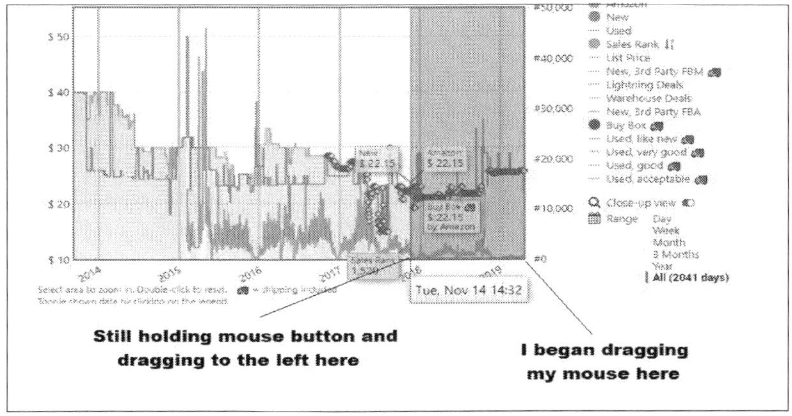

Assume I'm still holding down my mouse button and still dragging to the left as you study the image above. Although Keepa covered the 5.5-year timeline below the graph, you can see the graph's right edge is well into 2019 and so far, I've highlighted all of 2018 and 2019 without letting up on the mouse button.

I can continue dragging my mouse to select more of the graph until I get a little past 2017. That will select about two years. Releasing my mouse changes it to a two-year chart:

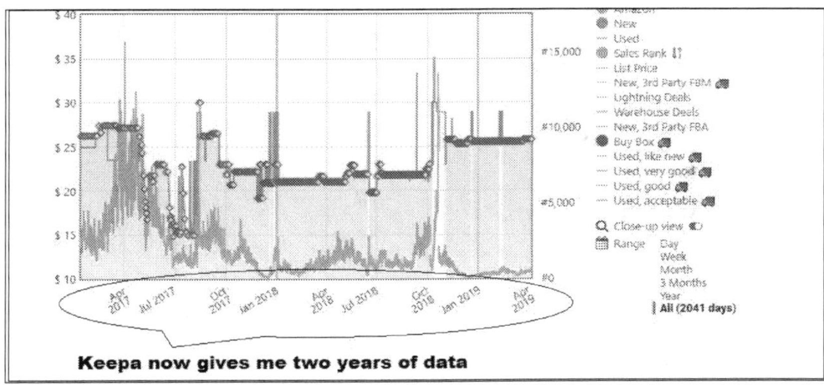

On your phone, you just pinch to zoom into the time frame you want to see, or reverse pinch outward to zoom out.

You therefore can go from a higher-level Keepa chart phone graph like this:

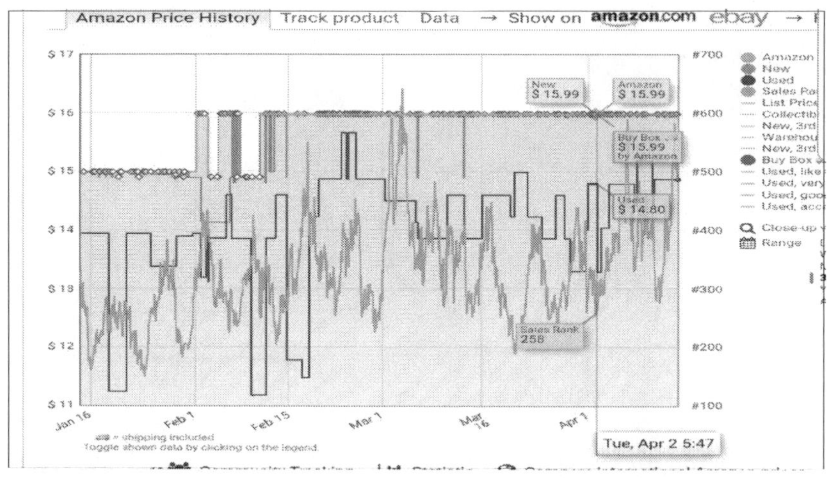

And zoom-in to a portion of the same graph like this one:

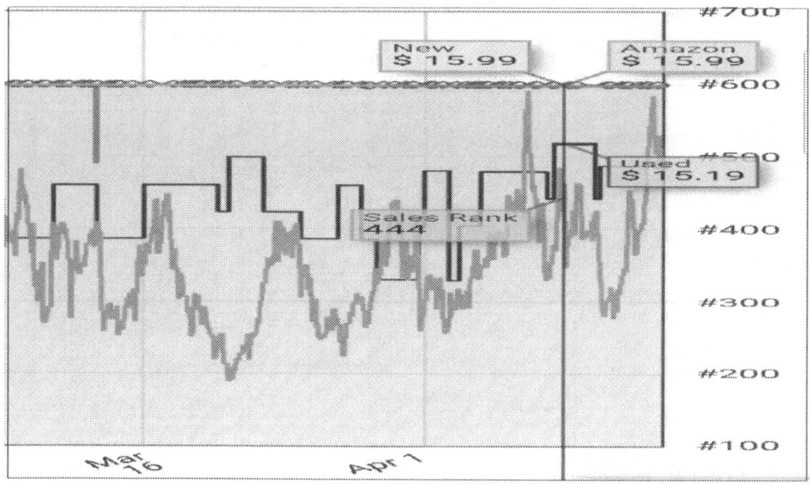

Knowing the Number of Sellers

The bottom Keepa chart shows the number of sellers on a listing. The number of sellers is called the *offer count*. If six sellers are selling an item, six offer counts display on the bottom graph. This "count" in no way indicates the number of items each seller has to sell. The offer count only tells us the number of competing sellers throughout a product's life.

Replen shoppers don't care as much about the number of sellers as most other RA shoppers except for slow-moving products. One thing we *do* care about is the seller count *trend*. If the purple line steadily increases with no dips, you should avoid that product. A growing number of sellers means more competition is jumping on the item. That often results in a price drop.

If the purple Offer Count line is steady, fluctuating up and down, or primarily decreasing, then test that product if the item is profitable and ranks well enough.

In the next chart, the purple Offer Count line fluctuates up and down from 7 to about 14 sellers. We would test the product if the top chart's profit and rank data were good:

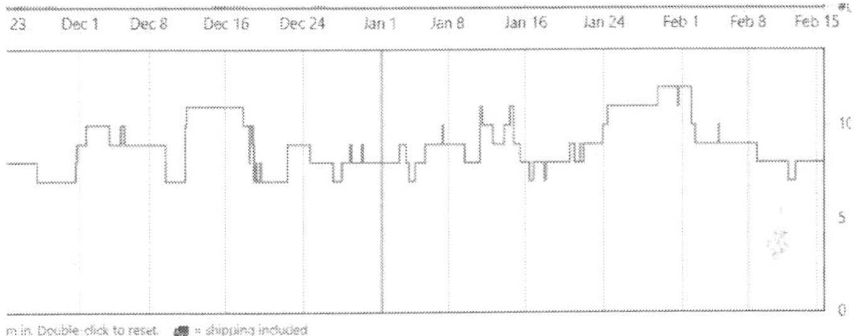

If there's consistently (over 3 months) one seller on a listing, don't test that item no matter how good things look. They're often a brand's listing or a private label product that we could have issues selling.

Here is such a chart:

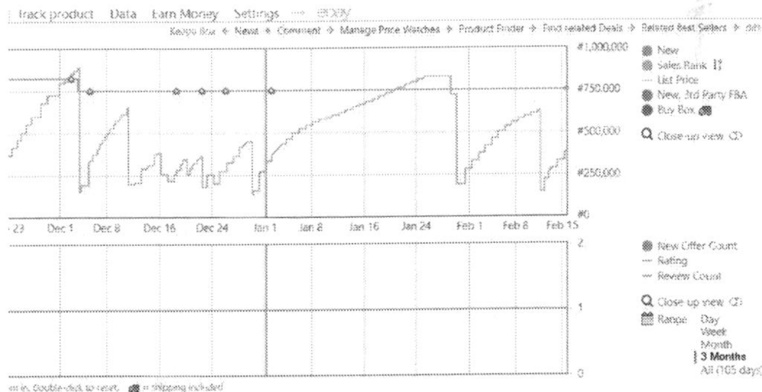

Some Implications of Amazon Selling an Item

When Amazon sells on a listing, the Keepa chart will be shaded orange as you saw. If Amazon is consistently on a listing, we normally won't buy that product because Amazon doesn't love to share the Buy Box. If Amazon has been on the product in the past for short periods of time, then we will test the product but only if they're not *currently* selling it.

An exception can occur where we test a few items even when Amazon consistently sells the product. Occasionally, you'll see the pink Buy Box line dip below the top of Amazon's shaded regions. This means Amazon prices higher than the current Buy Box owner. In this case, Amazon's giving other sellers the Buy Box some. We might test two to four of those to see if that trend holds.

Here's an example of such a chart:

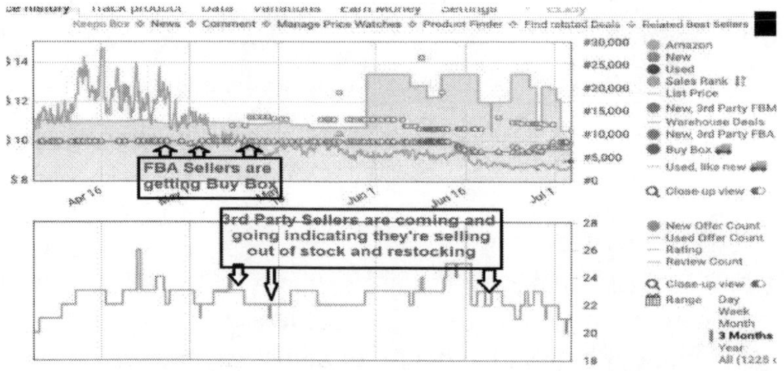

In the bottom chart, third-party sellers enter and leave the listing consistently. Therefore, they sell out and they or others restock and sell the item again.

Using the Statistics Box

Click the Statistics button and Keepa displays a table of information showing New Price, Used Price, Sales Rank and more. The New and Used information isn't important for replens. We sell nothing used. The New column includes Merchant Fulfilled sellers whom we aren't competing against. *Ignore those first two columns.*

Use the Statistics button to look at specific Sales Rank averages and the number of Sales Rank drops. The Drops give you an idea of how many sales per month (if it's not a fast-moving product). If it's a fast-moving product, the drops won't correlate to the number of sales because the sales rank will be low. The Average Sales rank helps you to confirm that the product is regularly selling as well. If the Drops show 50 per month, at least 50 sell (since 1 drop could be multiple items purchased). If Drops indicates around 10 sales monthly, you might test fewer, maybe three to five. The higher the Drops, the more an item sells and the more you can test confidently. Again, this changes depending on the price and number of sellers coming in and out of the listings.

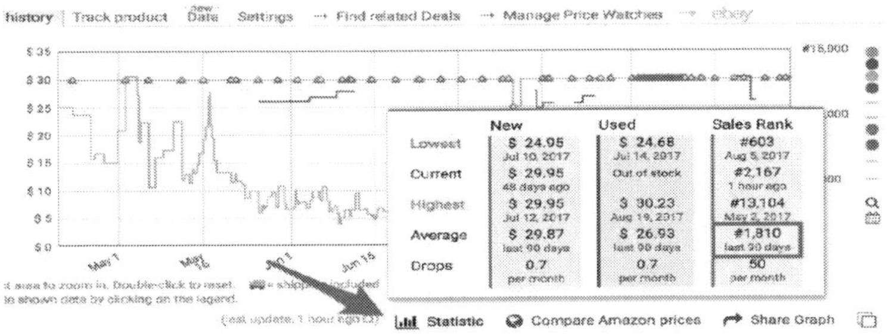

Some Buy / Don't Buy Examples

I'd like to close this Keepa overview with examples showing you products you would or would not buy. Sometimes Keepa deceives you until you learn to consider both the top *and* bottom charts as well as master how to monitor all the information I discussed earlier in this chapter.

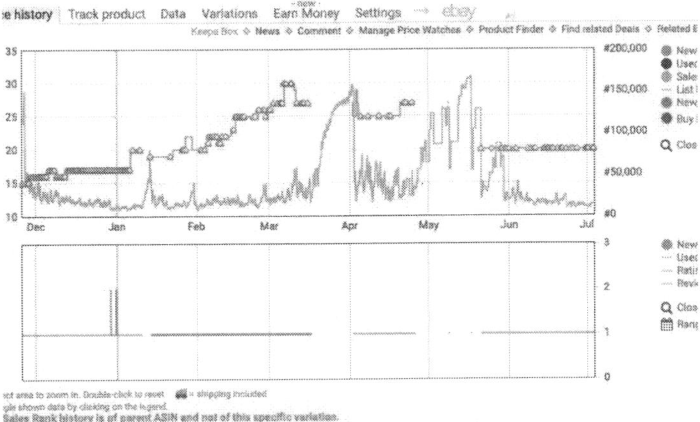

The product above has a great velocity. It frequently hangs around a low sales rank. The price began low at about $15 (the purple

New price line is often hidden by pink Buy Box icons when an item sells frequently; in this case, the New Price and the Buy Box price are often one and the same price). The price then rose to a high of about $30, and finally settled the last couple of months at $20.

It's nice to see the price showed no tanking effects because it never touched or dipped below the original price of $15. Depending on the price you can source this item, it may be profitable. But you don't look solely at the top chart.

This is a *don't buy* item!

The Offer Count shows only one seller is on the item except for two quick in-and-out appearances by a second seller. Such a seller chart can indicate this is a private label item or a brand's owner is selling the item. All other sellers are kept off the listing. The speed at which a second seller came and went, twice, is a strong indication they were hit with a removal notice and had to stop selling it.

Here's another example. Try to determine if the following represents a buy or don't buy recommendation:

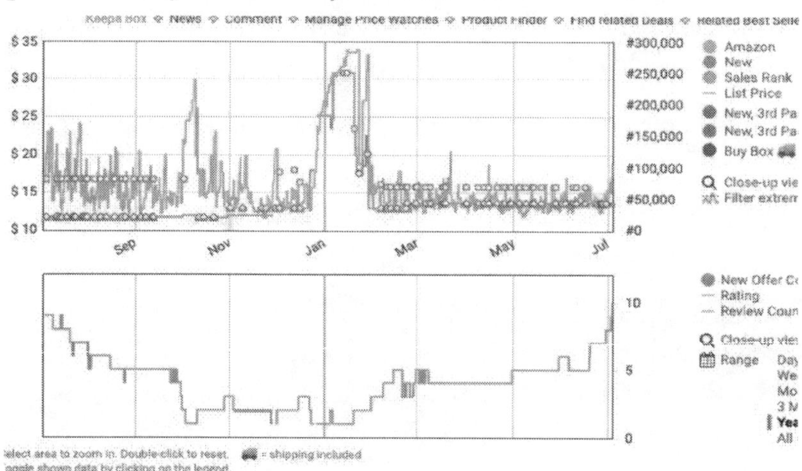

Notice the number of sellers is rising. Other resellers are finding and sourcing this product.

Still, we would test this item if we can buy it at a profitable price and the ROI meets our requirements. Sure, the seller count is going up, but it's rising slowly, and we see they dropped from the same level in the past.

Notice too that the Buy Box price is fairly stable around $12 and the Sales Rank consistently drops meaning it sells more items every month.

> **Note:** Ignore random, short-term Sales Rank and New Price spikes and drops. Those typically indicate just a data glitch or an oddity for that moment in time. It's a chart's trends you care about. The trend is your friend.

We would test four to six of these products if it's profitable at or around that $12 price point.

What does your analysis show here?

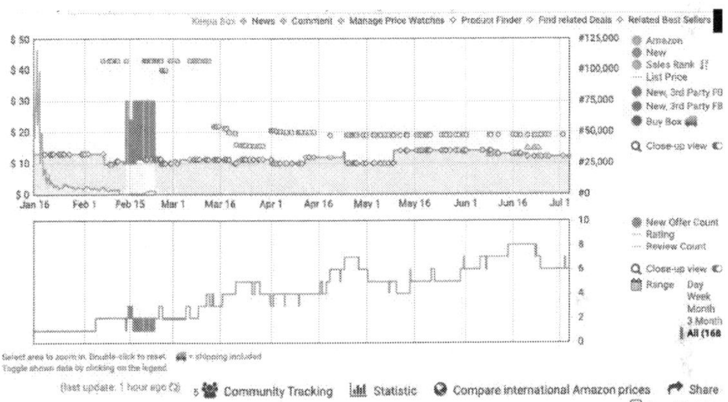

This item sells at a consistent price and has a magnificent Sales Rank approaching zero since way back on March first. In spite of the great rank and consistent price, we would *not* buy it. Amazon stays consistently on it and matches the Buy Box every time. You never see pink 3rd Party Seller icons dipping below Amazon's price. Nobody gets the Buy Box except Amazon most of the time.

To verify what we already see from the top chart, the bottom shows more and more sellers coming onto the listing with few dropping off. The few who drop off might just be pulling their slow-selling inventory to save long-term warehouse storage fees or Amazon is sharing the Buy Box but not at a significant rate.

If sellers got many sales, you'd see a more consistent rise and fall of the Offer Count line on the bottom chart. We don't want to source any product where Amazon gets stingy.

Would you source the next busy chart's product?

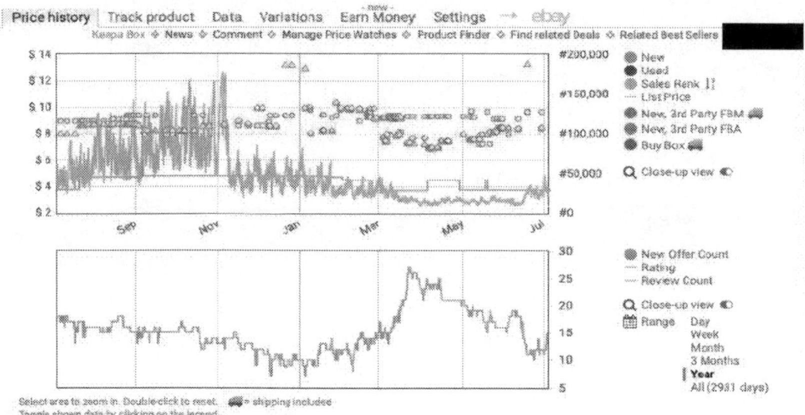

We would test six to eight of these.

The Sales Rank is steadily fluctuating, and the Buy Box price is fairly steady. It fluctuates so make sure it's profitable at the low price points, but the price hovers around a normal average price. In addition, the spike in sellers doesn't seem to be a problem. The seller count is rising but sellers have dropped off (probably sold out) along the way up and they are starting to drop off again as they have a few times before.

The incredible Sales Rank of close to zero indicates there's plenty of life and that it can handle more sellers. We would test from six to eight of these.

In the following chart, Amazon has been on the listing. Can you see where?

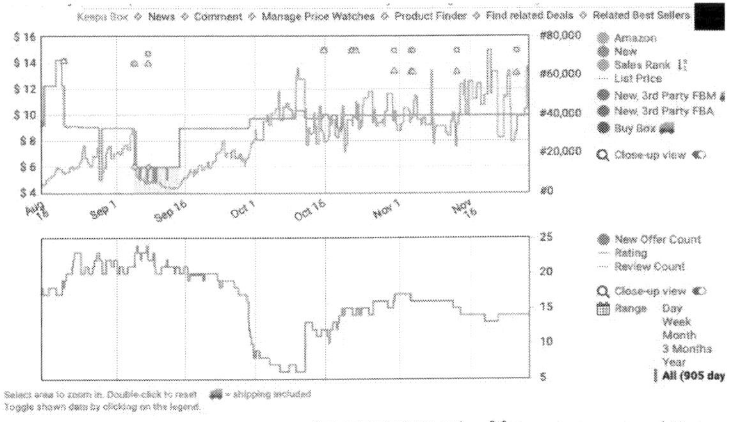

Here, we'd test it. Amazon was on the listing only a very short time in September. The Sales Rank consistently fluctuates (indicating good sales), and even though no pink Buy Box dots appear, the orange Triangles indicate that the FBA Price stays steady. Finally, the seller count fluctuates up and down.

Here, we would lower our test purchase though, to perhaps only four because the last month sales slowed, and the number of sellers stayed steady.

This is a nice chart:

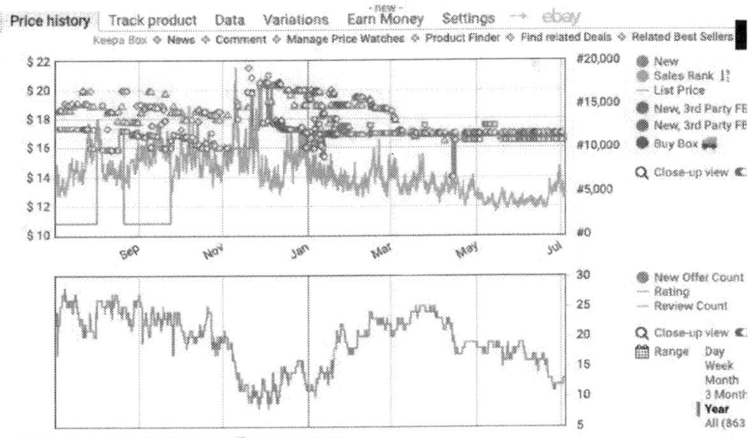

A lot of sellers move on and off. The Sales Rank fluctuates consistently, often in the good direction of down. The price stays fairly steady.

Does the following chart indicate a Buy or Don't Buy?

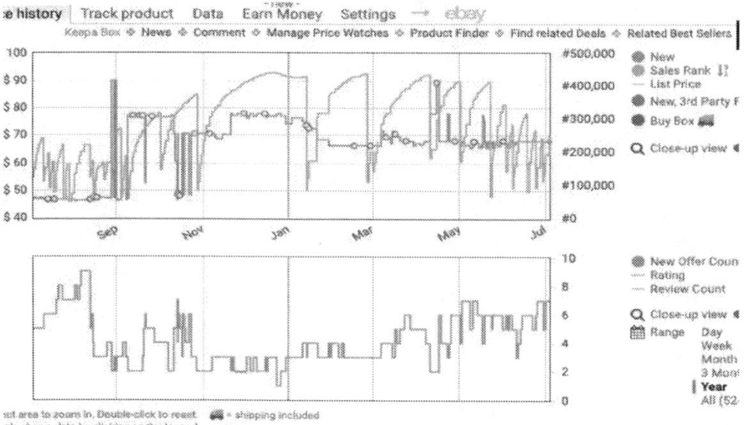

The sales are less frequent than many we've seen in this chapter. The Sales Rank line drops more dramatically and with more space between drops than the others. Still, the item does consistently sell. In addition, the last three months shows a steady selling price. Finally, the seller count fluctuates up and down regularly meaning many of the sellers have success.

We'd perhaps test three or four of these because it moves slowly at the moment, but it does move.

Not Every Seller on a Listing is Your Competitor

You rarely compete against *all* other sellers on an item.

For most listings, perhaps only 20% of sellers are priced near the Buy Box. A listing could have 25 sellers on it, but 20 of them are priced so far away from the Buy Box they aren't serious competition for those of us who price at Buy Box levels.

Those higher-priced sellers are holding out for the item to run out of stock. Or, perhaps they have so much inventory they don't adjust their prices as often as they should (they *should* use a repricer in most instances). Whatever the reason, you only compete against sellers priced near the Buy Box.

While the Amazon seller app lets you look at all the sellers on a listing and their current prices, Keepa shortcuts all this for us so we don't have to do that.

In the previous chart, the item's Sales Rank wasn't the best, so the sales velocity was slow. Not a lot of people sell a lot of that product each month. The up and down movement of the Offer Count line tells you all you need to know about how competitive the other sellers might be. Even though the item moved slowly, the number of sellers never hit 10 because sellers would sell out and new ones enter.

Perhaps some of the sellers, even 4 or 5 of them, may be priced so high that they aren't getting any sales during this chart's timeframe. You can check Amazon's list of current sellers and look at their prices but why do that when in one glance at the seller count line you know sellers come and go regularly?

Stay Positive!

At this point, you might have spent a lot of time analyzing why each chart was a Buy or Don't Buy. If you're brand new to Keepa then it does take a while to get a feel for the data.

You might recall Travis's *ACK!* admonishment that we never *ever* buy something to resell on Amazon without checking Keepa. That means you'll be looking at a *lot* of Keepa charts each and every time you go sourcing for new replens.

Yes, it may have taken you time to get through this chapter's charts, but there's not more to learn about Keepa to reach $100,000 in monthly sales. Be encouraged and not discouraged if Keepa seems tedious right now. Just check Keepa on every item when you first begin your hunt for replens. After only a day or two, you probably won't think twice about glancing at Keepa many times daily. All the elements you must check may seem daunting but they all work in tandem and you'll soon only have to glance at a chart to determine if the item's a buy.

Mastering *all* of Keepa's nuances takes far longer than a single chapter. It would probably take more than a single *book* to master every aspect! Rest easy knowing you don't have to do that. You need to know nothing more than you've just learned.

The final chart in this chapter follows. After you've used Keepa for a short time, you'll likely come to the same conclusion the Keepa masters would come to on this chart. That is, one *quick glance* tells you it's a Don't Buy.

Can you spot why?

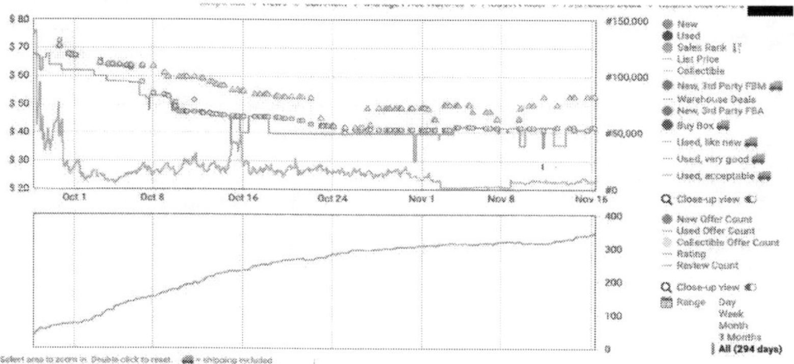

Even though the Sales Rank line is great and the price remained steady the graph's last half, the Offer Count rises with no decrease in sellers competing for sales.

With that growth of sellers, the price is sure to tank. This was an example of charts you'll often spot where something almost subconsciously triggers a Buy or Don't Buy decision.

Get the Free Keepa Updated Video Chapter

Since the publishing of the book, Keepa's had some minor changes to its design. Because of the changes, I made a free video for you that reviews the new look and feel of the software and Keepa's Chrome Extension.

You can watch the video and keep up with all the latest Keepa changes here:

askjimmysmith.com/free-keepa-chapter

Chapter 7
–
Finding Replens

You now have the tools to do the job.

It's time to get to work! The next 30 days, you want to list at least 30 replens in your inventory. The best way to teach you is to show you.

Let's find them together.

> "If you take action ten times a day while other people act on a new skill once a month, you'll have ten months of experience in a day, you will soon master the skill, and will, ironically, probably be considered 'talented and lucky.'"
> ~ Tony Robbins

Search Examples

I'll begin by showing you how to use your Amazon seller app in a store for sourcing replens. (You can also use your phone's seller app for OA. Of course, you have many other sourcing tools available when working on a laptop or desktop that can speed up your OA research.)

Let's say you're in the Sporting Goods department in the ping pong section. If you see the brand *Franklin*, search for *franklin ping pong*. Keep your initial search simple since we want to move from the general to the specific.

The iPhone Amazon Seller App
Shows Lists of Keywords

If you use an iPhone, when you start typing a search phrase into the Amazon seller app, a dropdown list of related items appears, such as:

franklin ping pong ball
franklin ping pong paddle
franklin ping pong net
franklin ping pong bag
and so on.

This doesn't appear on Android-based Amazon seller apps at the time of this writing.

The dropdown list is beneficial but not a must-have feature. Amazon is displaying a list of popular buyer searches related to your search phrase. Since resellers should think like buyers when searching, Amazon's displaying search phrases you can use to find as many listings as possible.

For Android users who want the same list, switch to your Amazon *Buyer* app to see a similar dropdown list.

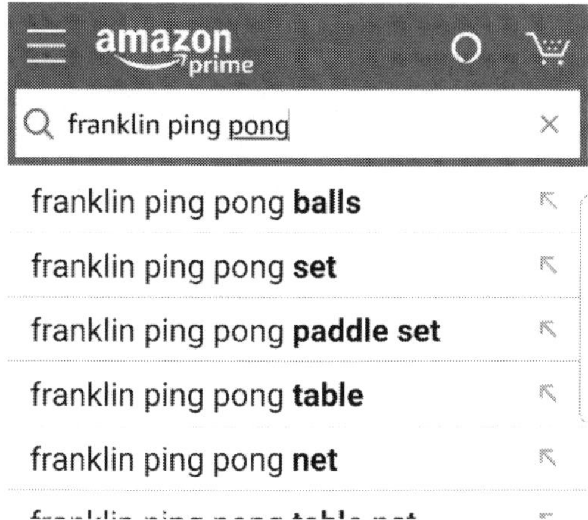

Notice that buyer searches are always basic: a brand and then the thing they're looking for. A simple general search shows the most possibilities in the aisle you're in. You'll still hunt for listings for specific things in front of you, but an initial general search gives you lots of options.

One of the first search results from the basic *franklin ping pong* search might be this:

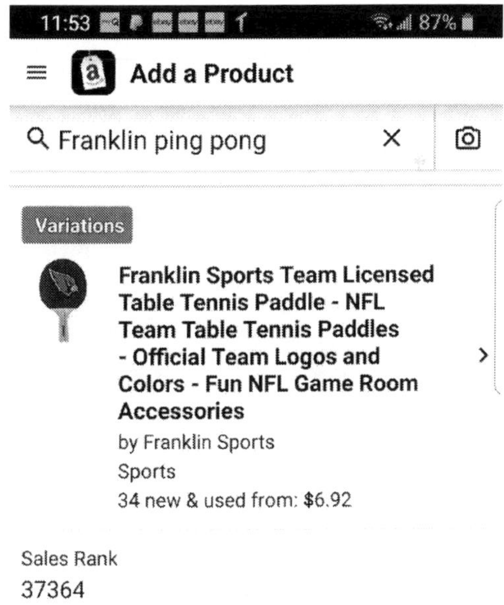

Notice you didn't have to type in all those words – *Franklin Sports Team Licensed Table Tennis Paddle – NFL Team ...* – to see the listing. You well understand now that lots of search results appear when you stay general.

Perhaps you're at Home Depot in the tools section. Husky is a Home Depot brand you'll run across. Type: *husky hammer* to see this:

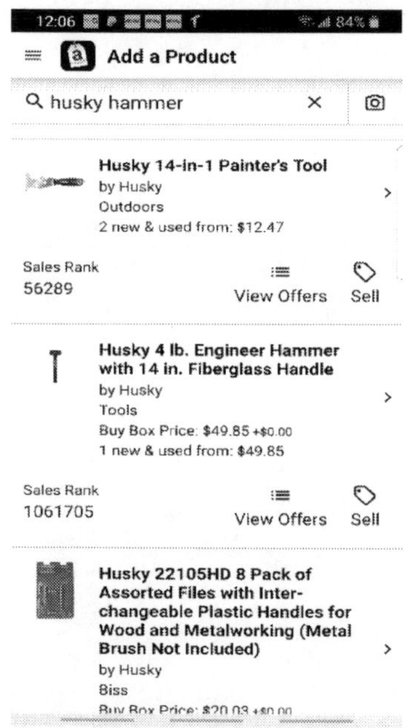

Even though the Seller app displays items unrelated to hammers, while I'm in the Husky area I could see if one of those other tools are worth sourcing. Obviously, a $12.47 selling price isn't high enough for our ASP of $15, but perhaps there's more to it than first appears. The Painter Tool's Sales Rank is great at 56,289. Lots sell.

You'd find those tools to see if they're profitable. (If the section you're in front of doesn't have the painter's tools, you can go look for them, but moving away from your current shelf isn't really the best use of your time, so you can search results from other areas later.)

Looking at the Painter Tool's Keepa graph below shows the price is $12.47 now, but it typically sells for about $15. Also, the number of sellers has dropped considerably which means it won't be highly competitive and might very well go up in price as the other sellers sell out. Depending on what you pay for the tool, you might want to test it to see how it does.

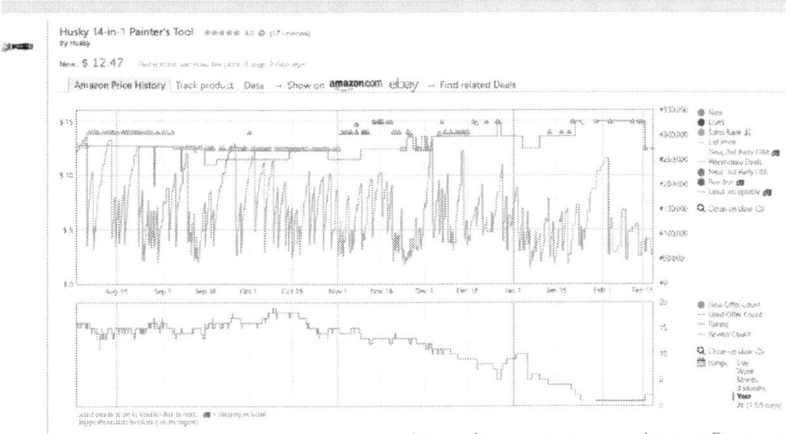

> **Note:** Technically, every time you first source something, you're testing it. Whether it looks like a great replen or an okay replen, the second month you will look at all replens to see which ones dropped off and which you source again.

Target has a private label brand of pet food called *Boots & Barkley*. Since so many kinds of pet food exist (dry, canned, snacks, special food for elderly and puppies, etc.), you begin with just *boots & barkley* to see what listings appear.

> **Tip:** I chose store brands for the past two examples because they reduce your competition. Resellers source at different stores depending on what they like to source and how they like to source. If you source the national brand Alpo dog food, you'll have more competitors because Alpo is sold almost everywhere. Only Target sells Boots & Barkley. This doesn't mean Alpo is less profitable; it may or may not be. Still, Boots & Barkley will be sold by fewer sellers than Alpo. Target is a national store, but unlike Alpo, Boots & Barkley isn't sold in other stores. We have a preference

> for store brands. We also prefer regional stores over national chains. Again, we'll source any brand at any store, but we find more opportunities when we source more limited brands and stores. That increases the odds of profitability and less competition.

As with most general search results, when I typed *boots & barkley* my seller app returned many listings. I've mentioned a few times a sort of sixth sense resellers begin to get over time. This isn't at all anything psychic but is nothing more than you getting better each time you analyze a product. Your skills improve each time. You get better and faster at finding replens and rejecting unprofitable items.

Here's the first screen from *boots & barkley*:

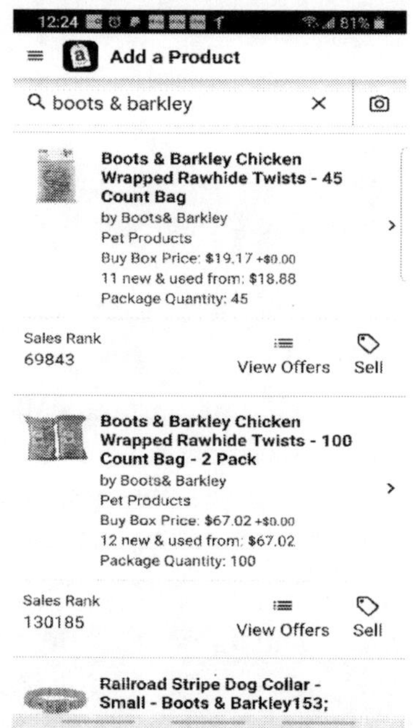

The first item looks like a possibility. The Buy Box is about $20 and the sales rank is good.

> **Note:** Remember, you only care about the Buy Box price. The *11 new & used from: $18.88* tells us mostly about Merchant Fulfilled (MF) sellers. FBA sellers rarely need to

worry about MF sellers. Many buyers who are members of Amazon Prime often limit their searches to FBA merchants only.

Look closer at that top item, the 45-count bag. Here's what you will do this time and every time: if you think $19.17 for 45 rawhide twists might be a little costly compared to the price you buy them at, especially at a 69,843 sales rank, look closer.

When we click that item, our seller app displays more detailed information:

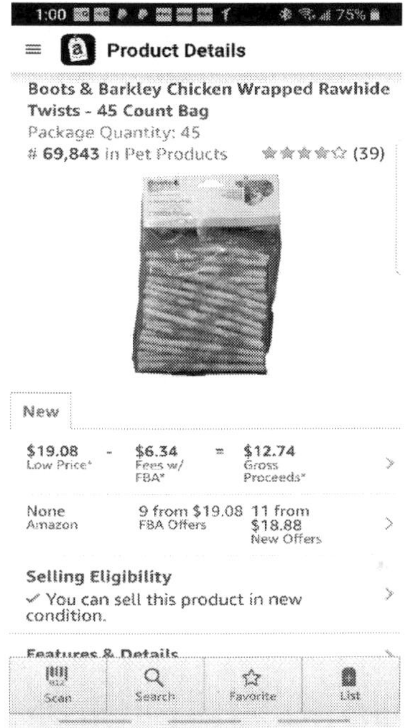

After Amazon's FBA fees, we get paid $12.74 for each bag we send in. Therefore, if you can buy these from Target for about $8 or less, you'll be meeting your profit, ROI, and ASP requirements. As you reach the higher stages of your replen business, you can pay as much as $9.50 because you'll better afford to reduce your average ROI.

Tip: Another good sign about this product is the review count. 39 reviewers reviewed it which means the listing has traction. As a general rule, every 100th buyer on average will review a product. Almost 4,000 have sold from this listing by that calculation.

Note: You'll sometimes run across something with no sales rank and Keepa also shows no rank. Many reasons exist. One is that the item is new or hasn't yet sold. Often, however, we find a listing without a rank that shows several reviews and a fluctuating seller count in Keepa. If the profit's there, we often test such products with no rank. The seller counts and the reviews tell us what a missing sales rank can't: the item sells. Most sellers avoid listings with no sales rank and that helps those of us who source it.

Is it profitable?

Only you can determine that. If the item costs only about $4 and is profitable, do you buy a few?

It sure looks like you do. Buy ten or more…

Nope!

Why?

ACK!

The more you fail to check Keepa, the more money you lose in bad buys and the more opportunity you miss in good buys you skip. (Yes, I know I've said this several times. I might even say it again!)

Checking Keepa for the past year shows the following chart:

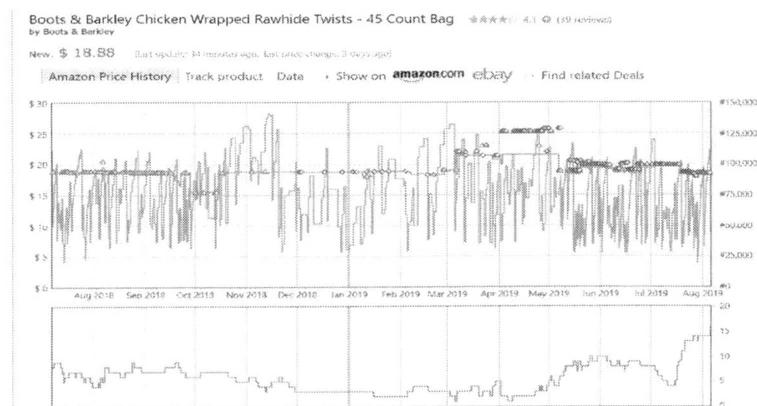

Note: Remember, Keepa defaults to 3-month timeframe but you will change it to a full year. (Assuming the product's sold for a year or more.)

The price fluctuated from the $18-19 range to a high of $25 for a short time and then back again, but it maintains a fairly stable price. All things being equal, you can make an educated guess that if you source a few of these and the price drops, you should ride out the drop for a few weeks; historically, it's reverted back to the $18-20 price range.

The problem is the rising seller count. This is a red flag. Yet, the item appears to be a winner. It *may* be a slower winner than other replens however with the competition increasing. Don't buy 10 or more, just get perhaps two to four if the purchase price makes it profitable.

On the same screen (repeated below), the second *Boots & Barkley* item caught my eye immediately. Such an item will often spark an interest in you too before long. It may or may not be a replen candidate, but the initial information we glean definitely requires a closer look.

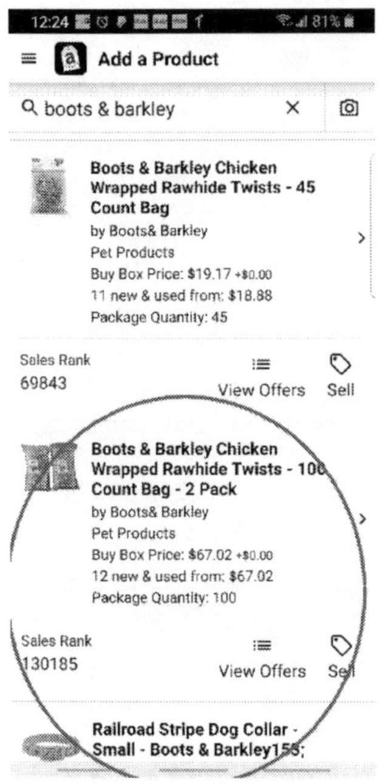

It's a 2-pack that sells for about $67. At this point, we don't know how heavy it is or if it'll ship as oversized items. We don't know the purchase price unless those Chicken Rawhide Twists happen to be right in front of us on the shelf. Still, its high-but-not-terrible sales rank keeps our interest.

There's something else that piques my interest and will start piquing yours when you see it. Pull out your Sherlock Holmes hat with me and let's consider something many resellers never think of. That is, the photo is good, but almost certainly not a professional picture. If the photo was as fancy as one that might appear in a Boots & Barkley catalog, the listing might have been created by the brand itself.

You can sell on listings created by brands if other sellers sell on it, but not being brand-created means we're probably on a listing some reseller made. Often, not always, reseller-made listings offer higher profits because the listing is more unusual than one the brand might create.

Being reseller created some time in the past is just one thing we like. We also like that it's a multi-pack of 2 bags. Brand owners don't create multipacks as often as resellers. Amazon doesn't sell on reseller-created multipacks and bundles as often as they sell on brand-created listings.

Our sleuthing means we'd look for this before going one-by-one on specific items. We'd source this if the buy cost is good and Keepa verifies things are fine.

Scrolling through more Boots & Barkley listings produces this 4-count bag.

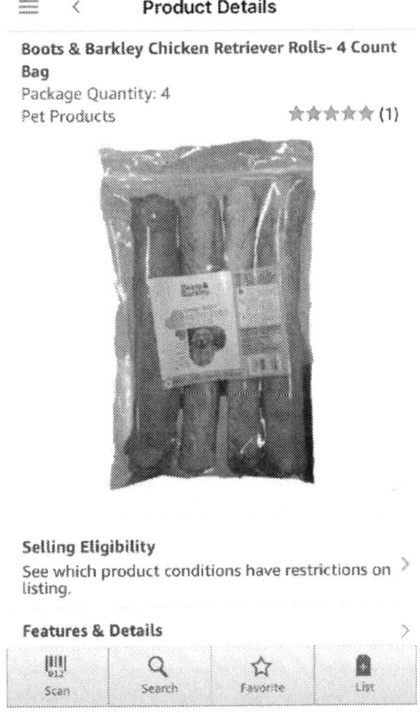

There currently is no rank and the product is out of stock, but the listing shows a buyer left a review. Therefore, it had some sales.

The only way to know if this is a candidate is to check Keepa. (You knew I'd say that, right?)

Here's the chart:

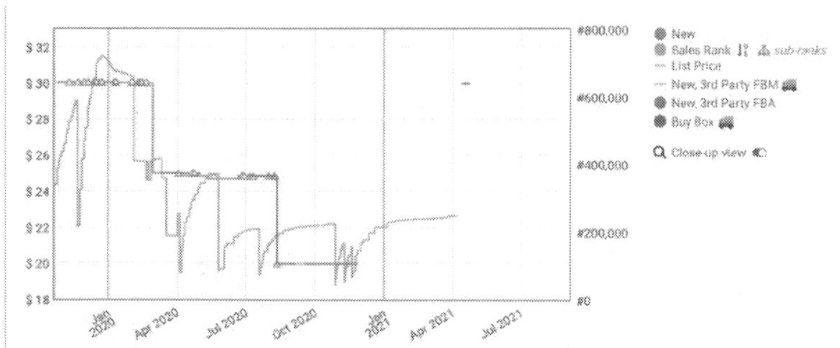

This doesn't sell often, but it sells. And when it was in it briefly came back in stock between April 2021 and July 2021 it most likely sold immediately since the Buy Box line appeared and disappeared very quickly.

The $20-$30 selling price seems high which is good for us. (I know nothing about Boots & Barkley, but the price would make me analyze this listing's 4-count bag further.)

You can tell that when the price was lowered to $20 it sold much quicker at the end of that period because it was a much more reasonable price. Most likely I'd come in at $30 on this listing, but as long as I can make money at $20, I'd be willing to slowly drop the price until we started making sales.

> **Note:** Newcomers make sourcing harder than they ever should. Once you know how to get around your seller app and check a few things on Keepa, the review count, and pricing, your sourcing decision comes down to common sense. If you can sell this item profitably, but at a price less than the current $30 price, source three or four, maybe more if the profitability is superb at the lower price, and test if your price drop sells these faster. You're not tanking the price (although the current seller may disagree, if there is one), you're making the price slightly more reasonable to increase possible sales.

Here's a replen we'd buy. It doesn't sell often but it sells. We only need a handful, even a single digit's worth of sales each month, especially given its higher selling price than our suggested $15

ASP. We don't want to compete against lots of sellers. We want to find an item that's probably a little overpriced but that still sells. In this case, we would be reviving this listing since there are no other sellers currently on it! We will be the only option! Once listed, we might bring the price down to a slightly more reasonable level to get more sales. Not only do we, but all sellers who joins in our price range sell more. The more an item sells, the lower the sales rank and the faster the velocity. Amazon rewards better selling products by raising their rank when people search for similar items. You would then test a higher price to see if you can maintain sales as the overall sales increase. New sellers on this listing will take a while to realize they should source it too. The fact you slightly decrease the price now *could* turn this into a major seller a few months from now and you'll ride the wave up.

> **Note:** Can *you* create that demand and therefore a fantastic replen winner only to see it tank months later if many sellers sell on the listing? Sure. That's okay. That's actually great! You're not trying to create an unprofitable listing, but until it does, you benefit from its new success. Items drop off as you know.

Again, this all becomes common sense. You're smart enough to use sense when sourcing as long as you first rely on your seller app's and Keepa's initial data. Depending on the numbers, if this product isn't good enough to expect ten sales each month, it might be good for two or three. That decreases your required average of ten sales per item each month. This means you need other replens that sell more. Still, at this item's selling price of $20 or higher, your ASP and maybe ROI averages go up making it easier to hit the next stage even if you sell fewer than 10 monthly.

This is why if an item shows great profit and ROI, but might only sell two or three monthly, it very well can fit into your required returns and keep you on track to hit the next stage on time.

No matter how good the numbers look, you can't foresee everything. Check each month to see if last month's items held up well enough to source again. If so, you have a true replen for now.

If the first month's sales disappoint, then it drops off this month and you'll replace it with another next month.

A Regional Store's Examples

So far, I've shown you examples from a Home Depot private label store brand (Husky) and Target (Boots & Barkley). Now let's look at some examples from Trader Joe's. It's still a regional store because Trader Joe's isn't available everywhere yet.

> **Tip:** The more variety your replens have, the more consistent your replen sales should be. Consistency is what we love about replens. We just want a few sales, from a growing number of items, every month. The more consistent the sales, the fewer drop-offs we'll have and the less we must work to replace those that drop out.

When you type *Trader Joe's* into your iPhone seller app or your computer browser, you'll see all sorts of items dropdown that buyers want. Many seasonings appear in the dropdown list, so this is a clue that the *seasoning* might be an opportunity for us. (Again, Android users can see this dropdown from typing *Trader Joe's* in the Amazon Buyer app.)

Type *trader joes seasoning* to see many listings. (Some display variations meaning different quantities and possibly different flavors sell in the same listing). If you click on a variation listing, you'll be able to scroll through the variants of this seasoning.

Here's a possible set of listings that appear when you type *trader Joe's seasoning*:

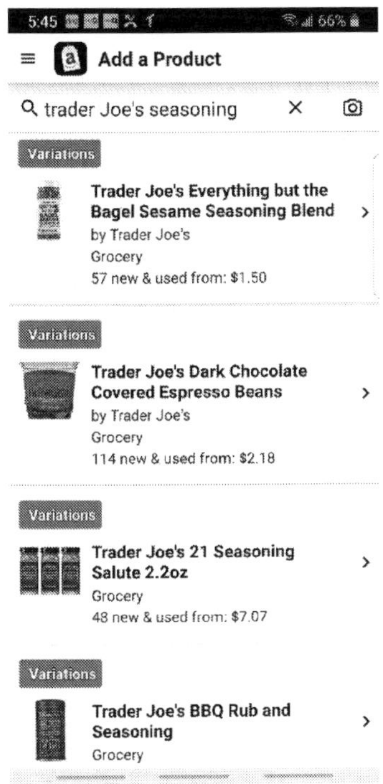

As you scroll through the search results, you'll see many multipacks selling. Replens sellers love multipacks and you'll find plenty to choose from here to check.

> **Tip:** At the time of this writing, the Trader Joe's brand doesn't sell its products on Amazon. Most listings you see will be seller-created. This keeps the biggest seller, the owner, off the product. Fortunately, it also keeps Amazon off many times too.

Let's look at a few examples.

Here's a screen for Trader Joe's 21 Seasoning Salute 3-pack:

This 3-pack currently sells for $14.14 and has 19 FBA sellers. Amazon doesn't sell this. The 226 reviews demonstrate it's sold well for a long time. The rank of 9,331 is superb. I don't know what these generally cost in the store, but if profitable, you'd look this up on Keepa to find this:

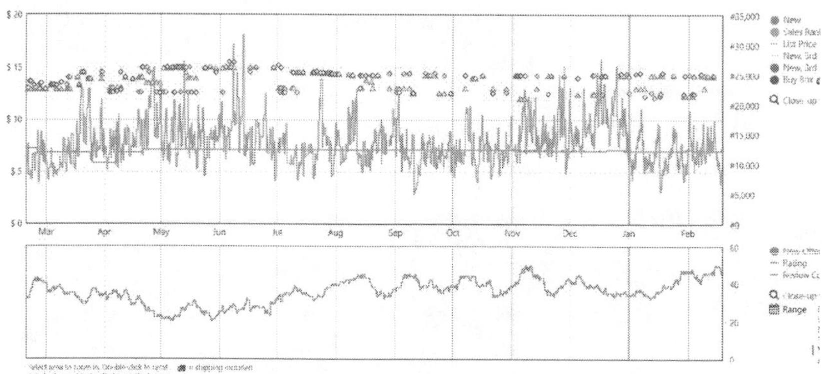

Keepa shows an up and down seller count. Even though the seller count is relatively high, it's been that high before and has always moved up and down nicely implying that many sellers are getting sales. The sales rank fluctuates heavily, but the price remained between $12 and $15.

In situations where the price routinely fluctuates between values, always base your sourcing on the lower price range. If these are profitable at $12, then if and when the price rises to $15, it's added profit for you and raises your ASP and average ROI as long as the higher price remains.

If the $12 price brings down your average ROI to below 40%, perhaps watch for the rising price again. When it hits $13 or $14, the ROI may be more your current average range. Or, once you hit enough sales to reach Stage Three or Stage Four, the lower price range will fall more within your ROI and ASP and you can source it if the numbers remain constant.

You're still in Stage One, so don't accept ROIs below 40%. You'll make more bad buys in the beginning than later. You have less room for those extra mistakes because you have fewer sales and less money coming in to buy new inventory. Stage One's stricter profit requirements ensure that a few bad buys won't affect your overall income as they would with tighter profit margins. You might be able to skimp on estimated sales of 10 items monthly for items whose selling price and ROI are high, but never cheat on your minimum ROI in the beginning.

Along the same lines, always seek faster moving items when you can. That higher velocity helps build your early cashflow faster. You'll put that quicker cashflow back into new inventory.

> **Note:** I'm not concerned with you knowing about Trader Joe's 21 Seasoning Salute's profitability of course. I want you to master this process. If you were in the Trader Joe's seasoning aisle and ran across this seasoning, your general search of *trader joes 21 seasoning salute* would display this same listing. Finding the listing from the product *or* from a general search ultimately results in the same analysis. When you're in the store, there's no magic and nothing special; you just keep checking product after product, over and over, just as you're seeing here.

Next is the Amazon Seller app's screen for Trader Joe's Everything but the Bagel Sesame Seasoning 2-pack:

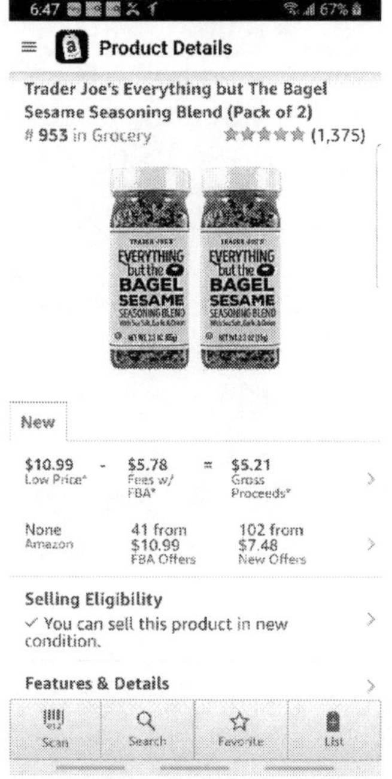

Nobody can argue with the rank. The number of 5-star reviews is outstanding. This will bring down your ASP, but that's less critical than violating ROI right now because other items you source can quickly bring your ASP up. If the cost enables you to consider this 2-pack profitable at this stage, you then do exactly what you always do - check Keepa:

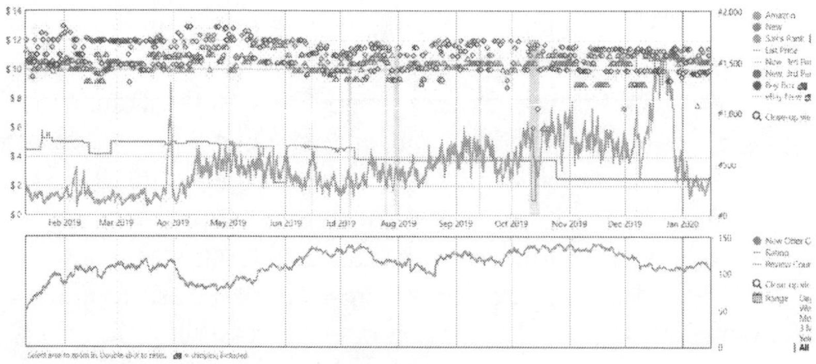

Amazon has come and gone on this listing, but Amazon's presence is so small that there's no reason to consider them a threat.

Sellers go up and down but do fluctuate. The price is consistent between $10.50 and $13 or so. $2.50 to $3 is a rather large price swing for this price point but again it's consistent. If the margins are there for you on the lower end, you might test it. If not, you might file this one away to check in 6 months when your ROI requirements change and when this 2-pack might even be more profitable.

Looking around you, your searches get more specific. You might type *trader joes everything but the bagel seasoning* to locate listings that didn't appear before. Add *bundle* and then perhaps *variety* to the search. The more varied a bundle is, assuming your profit requirements are met, the less competitive that listing will be. If resellers must gather and bundle different products, even when from the same store, they're less likely to jump on a bundle.

You'll find the seasoning bundled with Trader Joe's Chile Lime Seasoning Blends for example. You'll find multipacks of 10 or more seasonings and listings with various seasoning sizes. As popular as this seasoning is, being Trader Joe's top-selling item month after month, you're almost sure to find a listing you can sell on profitably.

> **Tip:** When looking at any product that sells well, such as Trader Joe's Everything but the Bagel Sesame Seasoning, keep looking for more and more listings. Its popularity makes just about any listing it's found on sell better than it otherwise would.

That one product might result in five or ten other replens! This is exactly the way you begin to skyrocket the number of replens you find each month. When you must find 30 replens in 30 days, and one day you find five or more, the rest of your month is easier and less stressful. If you maintain the same pace, however, you'll find more than 30 replens that month. Everything like this you can do lets you hit the $100,000 in monthly replens faster. Yay!

Keep Your Eyes Open

As you scout for replens, you're always looking for listings that sell for more than the item probably sells for in your store. Always focus on your numbers. You might find a 2-pack of Suave shampoo that has a great rank and is an extra-high selling item that turns out to be unprofitable because the purchase price is higher than you expected.

You'll still be on the lookout for these high-value listings as you scroll through products. The general results save you time over checking every listing you see.

And with everything, you'll begin to see these situations more and more often as you hone your skills and invest time into doing the work.

Chapter 8

–

Online Arbitrage and Replens

Although RA is our preferred method of sourcing, we use OA too. Some resellers prefer OA for all their replens inventory. That's great. You'll approach both OA and RA with the same profit requirements Stage One requires. All OA analysis is basically identical to RA.

The biggest difference is that you're searching for replens online and not in a store aisle.

OA Searching

Typically, I start by going to a store's website and there I type a brand name. All the RA tips apply to OA. Therefore, a regional store's site is *generally* less competitive than a national store. Having said that, we source many items at national chains, but regional stores improve the odds that fewer resellers will be on a listing.

Whether regional or not, store brands as opposed to national brands also help to reduce the number of competitors on a listing.

This means if you're on the Lowe's website, items you find for Black & Decker will have more sellers than the Lowe's house brand Kobalt because Lowe's isn't the only chain to sell Black & Decker.

Typing *Kobalt* on Lowe's website, therefore, might produce this:

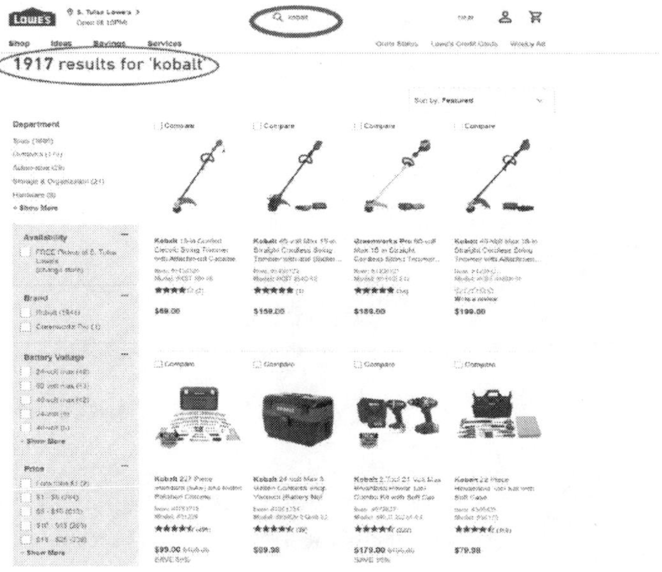

One expects such Lowe's searches to produce many oversized and heavy items. That's what we see here. The trimmers are going to be too long to fit in standard boxes. Their size will incur oversized shipping fees when we send them to Amazon, when we're charged FBA storage fees, and then from Amazon to the buyer taken out of our FBA costs. Many tools will be heavy which further reduces potential profits.

Should you avoid some brands and categories because of size and weight? Absolutely not. First, not all Kobalt tools will be oversized or heavy. Those that are might offer enough profit that we don't care about the extra costs. We don't want to assume too much when sourcing. We're also realistic that a lot of the items will be prohibitive because of the nature of tools and the equipment used with tools.

Remember that *most* items at any website or store we source at will be unprofitable. Otherwise, I'd want you to find 30,000 replens in 30 days, not just 30! This is why patience and mindset are critical; if sourcing were ultra-easy, everybody would do it.

Like RA, once you get a search going on the website, switch to Amazon.com and look for the same brand. Perhaps you'd type *kobalt* or *kobalt tools* to display some Amazon products and start the replens search.

Here's a screen of Amazon listings found by searching for *kobalt*:

Note: Your own Amazon results will always look different from mine. Between the time I save screens and the time when you search, Amazon will find a different set of products, with some overlap. Products come and go, products are sourced and then not sourced, prices change, bundles get created.

That's good! That's exactly why I can find things to source today and when you read this book, you'll find things I never saw. Replens will never all be taken.

Warning: I use Chrome extensions you may or may not use. That might make my screens look slightly different from yours also.

Speaking of extensions, one I suggest you install now is called *DS Amazon Quick View.* Every time you search on Amazon, DS Amazon Quick View displays each item's rank (highlighted in pink on the items above) and the number of FBA sellers for each item. This speeds up your sourcing because you can quickly eliminate high ranks or items with a hundred or more competing FBA sellers.

When the search results appear, scroll through them. Look for items that are priced high, or that you think might be high for the listing's product. As with RA, seek active listings that might have extra profit potential.

In the lower-left hand corner of the previous search results is a Kobalt 24-volt brushless motor cordless combo kit for $229. The rank is high at almost 400,000 but it was winter when I searched. Sales might pick up in spring. We could check Keepa, but generally we hold off on Keepa until we see if we can buy the item profitably.

Switching back to Lowes.com, if we type a general phrase for that item, such as *kobalt brushless motor combo kit*, we find these results:

A kit almost like the one Amazon showed appeared, but it's the same price as that Amazon listing *and* it comes with an extra item (a soft case).

It's too early to move away from Lowe's. Just because we found one specific item that's not worth messing with, and possibly many more items in that category that are going to be too heavy, oversized, or just not priced low enough to make money, we don't want to assume too much. Still, sometimes we can get bogged down in a category that isn't going anywhere.

You can change tactics and stay in such categories a little longer.

Click the Sort dropdown list on a Lowe's search to switch from the default *Featured* products to a different order of results. We can search again for *kobalt tools* but change the sorted results to *Price Low to High*:

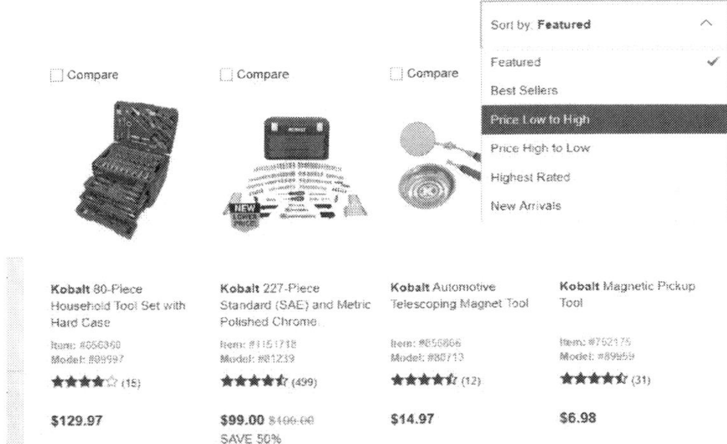

By sorting this way, you'll find smaller, less expensive items that might be easier to deal with in FBA. Bundled listings of the cheaper, and therefore usually lighter items, might display unique, low-competing listings to sell on.

Below are the first few listings that appear on a Price Low to High Price sorted display:

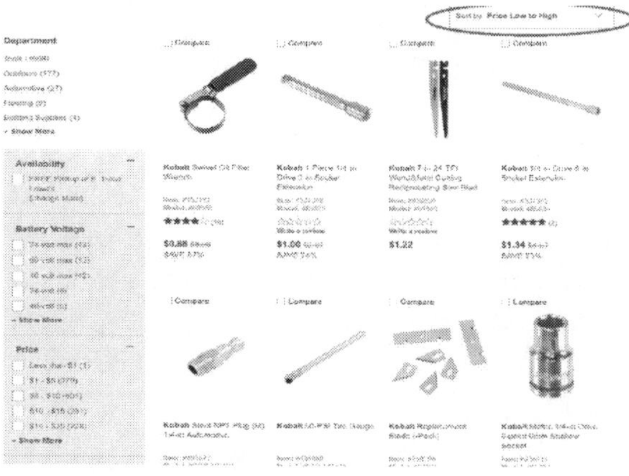

I know from lots of sourcing that stores such as Lowe's and Home Depot sell thousands of small, low-priced items. Think nuts, bolts, individual couplers, and small PVC connectors.

Just about any search from Low to High Price produces those kinds of items. Although many can be profitable, often in bundles, going through them can take quite a while with a low percentage of finds. Lowe's sells hundreds of different nuts, bolts, screws, and nails.

On this specific kind of store, I bypass checking most of these tiny parts that appear often and early in Low to High Price sorted search. I scroll through several pages quickly looking at each and every page noticing when I see something other than the cheap, tiny parts.

For example, amidst the bolts and connectors, the very first page of the sorted *kobalt tools* search produced this 2-piece screwdriver set:

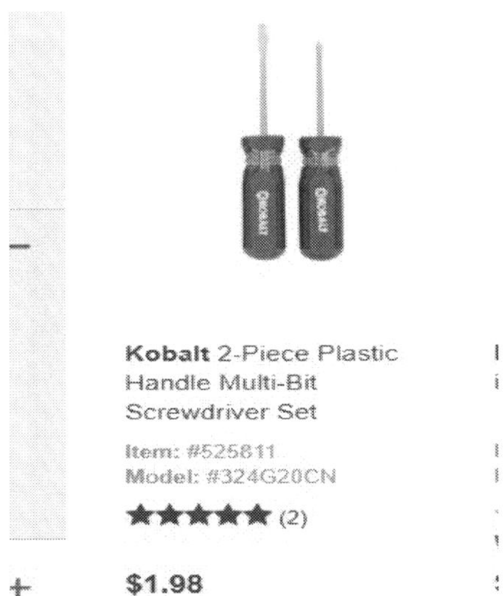

$1.98 might be a low purchase price compared to what sellers offer it for on Amazon. Who knows? We don't know but we know how to find out, right?

To find listings with this screwdriver set, you don't want to type the full Lowe's title into Amazon. That's not starting with a general enough search. We'd search for *kobalt 2-piece screwdriver.* Even though that's about as general as we can get, it produced only one result here:

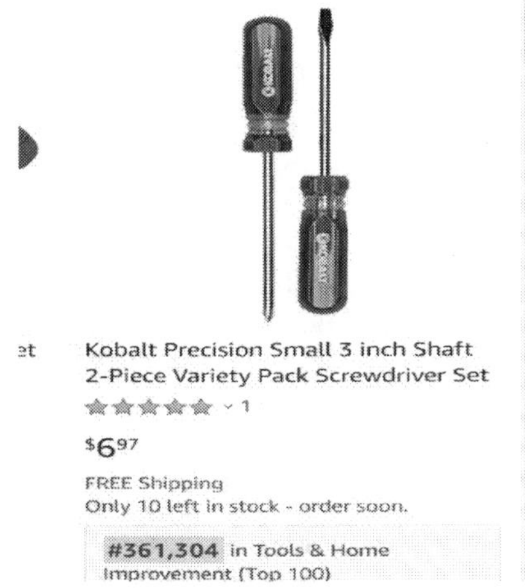

The rank is high, but you've seen we're not afraid of a relatively high rank because we only need to sell a small number each month. Still, the Amazon price of $6.97 can't produce anywhere close to our required profit and ROI after Amazon fees. We'd return to Lowes.com to scroll more.

> **Tip:** If you ever can't locate a website's product on Amazon by searching for it, right-click the item's image on the Lowe's or other website and select Search Google for Image. Google uses the picture to look all over the Internet for that image. Sometimes, a profitable Amazon listing appears that you couldn't find with a text-based search. Perhaps the listing was a bundle that had the screwdriver set as one of the images but didn't use all the words in your general *Kobalt 2-piece screwdriver set* search.

Searching through the 2-piece screwdriver set listings on Amazon only produced the match that you saw above, but this listing appeared a row or two later:

Kobalt 35-Piece Double Drive QL3 Quick Load Variety Screwdriver Set

69

$65.79

Get it as soon as **Sat, Feb 22**
FREE Shipping by Amazon
Only 1 left in stock - order soon.

That caught my eye because of the high price of $65.79. It doesn't seem like a lot of product for the price Amazon's listing sells it for. Again, I have no idea if the price is low, fair, or high, but it stood out so I took a quick look into it.

The rank is 168,341 in Tools & Home Improvement which is more than good enough for a replen. Let's see what the price is on Lowe's by searching there for this specific item:

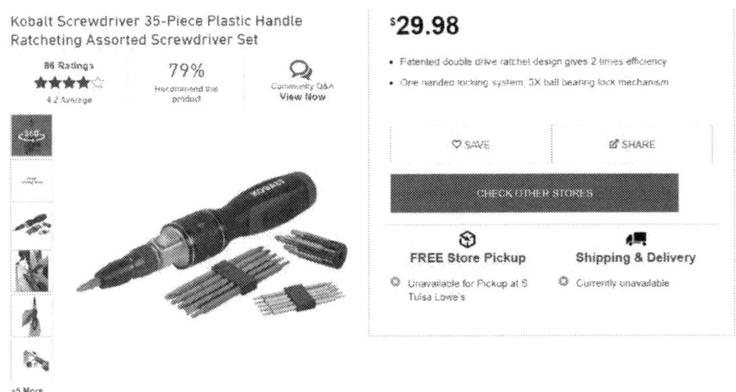

This has replen possibilities. We'll go farther.

I entered the cost and sales price figures into an FBA calculator and produced these results:

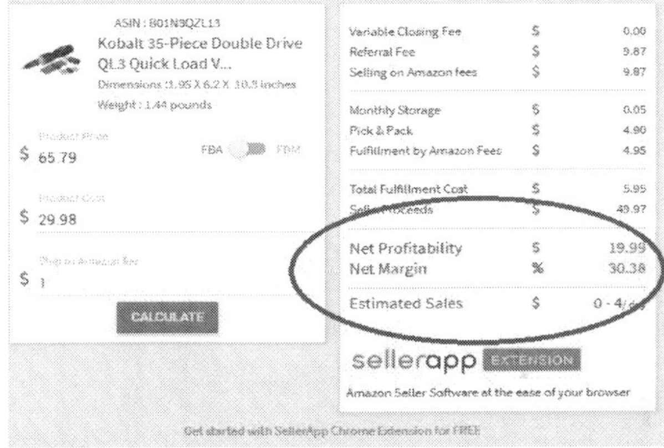

Wow!

These numbers are superb with an ROI is of 67% ($19.99/$29.98). This Kobalt set is a replen that one would hope lasts a long time.

What does Keepa say? As you know, Keepa always has the final say:

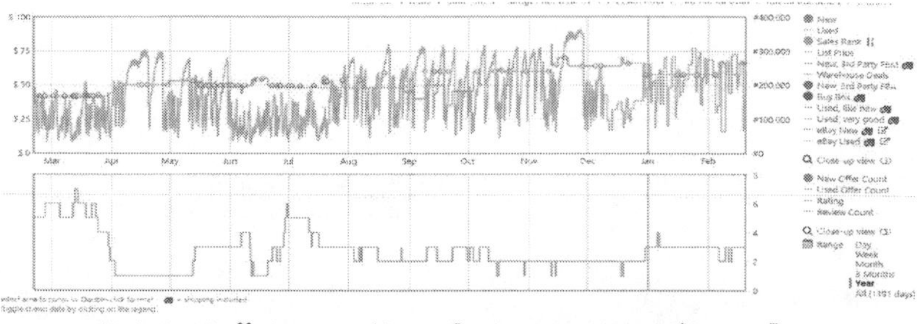

We've seen far worse Keepa graphs. The competing seller count is low and sellers have been moving on and off the listing nicely. The sales rank shows constant sales. The price remains fairly steady, actually increasing the past several months. The general price trend doesn't look as though it'll stop soon.

Keepa likes this product for a replen.

Continuing the Trail

This kind of online replen searching is more random than an in-store RA search will be.

In stores, you'll often perform "reverse searches" as I've shown you where you type a general brand or item search phrase to see if any listings pop up that match things in front of you. While in the aisle, however, you'll also search for the actual products to find as many profit opportunities in front of you that you can.

OA sourcing can be one of those times when you don't want to check each item on the screen for profitability. Instead, what I often do is look through some of the items for unexpected listings that are still the Kobalt brand but don't really fall into the category of search I did. Many of them will be the tiny, one-bolt kinds of items but other keywords might spring up you can search for. In scrolling through the previous Lowe's search screen, I saw the phrase *polished chrome.*

Do any polished chrome items offer replen opportunity? I don't know. But I know how to find out and so do you.

A *kobalt polished chrome* search produced this listing:

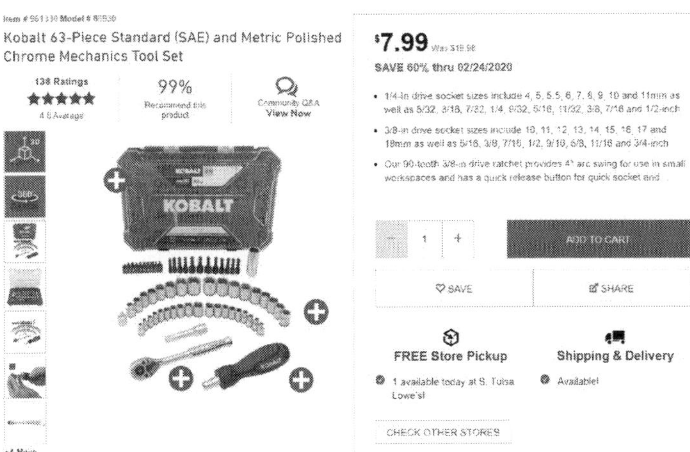

That caught my eye because even though I'm no expert on tools, it looks like a nice set that costs me only $7.99 to buy.

> **Note:** This set happens to be on sale. You might recall me saying earlier that we don't plan to base our replen inventory on sale items. Still, they *can* be worth testing. Sales are often repeated. Walmart *Rollback* sales often stick around for months. This sale had a specified end date of February 24th, so it may not end up being a repeatable profit. Still, if it's profitable now, we don't want to just bypass the money. It may not be a replen but it can make money. Let's see if it's profitable. I would take the time to do this given the amount of items in the picture versus the price it all costs. We would add it to our replens list for the month. Next month, if the sale does actually end and the price is too high to source, we'll drop it as a replen but perhaps add it to a list we check the first of each month to see if it goes back on sale regularly for a purchase then. Even if a replen only works quarterly, we want it in our mix.

I looked on Amazon for this set and saw this:

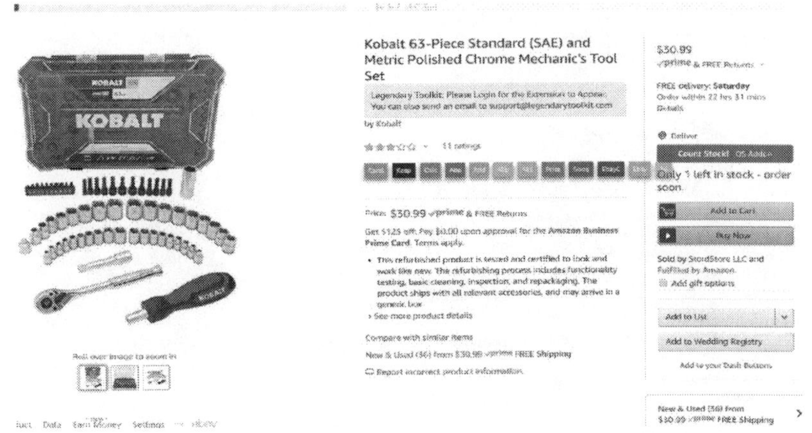

Hmm… Almost too good to be true. Not only does Amazon's Buy Box show $30.99 for this $7.99 set from Lowe's, the listing describes a refurbished product according to the description. You'll be coming in with a brand-new item and should easily be able to sell it for $39.99 or more. You may have to create a new listing for the new item, but you can use all the data here except for removing the "refurbished" bullet point.

Here's the must-see Keepa chart:

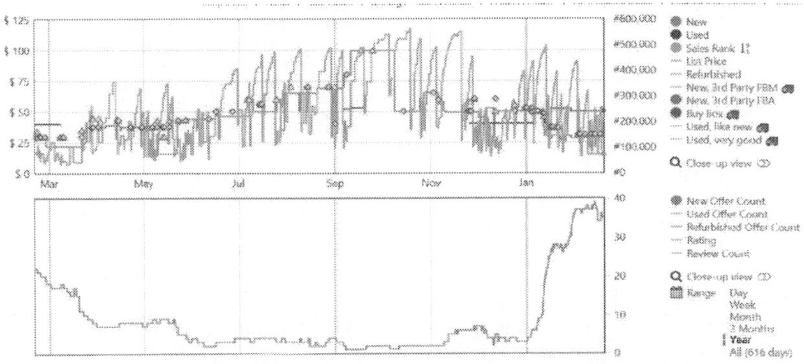

Finally, we see that this isn't a perfect product, but some opportunity could be here.

The immediate warning is the rise in the number of sellers from under 10 to about 35 currently. Even with that rise, the price still hovers around $30-$50 and Amazon isn't on the listing. The rank is a little high and yet these sell consistently.

Again, *this is for a listing that's refurbished.*

I like to show you exceptions and not listings that always work out cleanly. My guess is many of these sellers are selling brand new items and not caring that the description is for a refurbished product. No buyer will complain when he thinks he bought a refurbished tool but got a new one instead.

You could sell on this listing without creating a listing. As I suspect most of these sellers are doing, you'd sell brand new sets on the refurbished listing.

Given the number of sellers and given we don't like to create listings for replens, we'd probably test three or four of these because they show lots of life. It may be the *end* of its profitable life with all the new sellers and the sale ending soon, but we won't know for sure without testing.

Next month, we can hope the situation remains the same because this is a high dollar profit item if the price remains stable.

Another Way to Find OA Possibilities

Look around your house at things your family uses. Far more OA opportunities exist all around than you might expect.

When I just walked through the house, I saw Gain dryer sheets.

The box has the weight, the number of sheets in each box, an *Island Fresh* scent, and additional information that distinguishes this box from other Gain dryer sheets available.

What would I type into Amazon to see if any might look profitable?

Gain dryer sheets

Remember, we start with the general and drill down to specifics. I don't care about looking for *island fresh scent* yet. I want to see lots of listings appear with all sorts of dryer sheet combinations.

You don't have to be a dryer sheet expert to look for listings that appear to be expensively priced. Scroll looking for high-priced listings, look for bundles and multipacks, and even look for pictures that aren't perfect, such as ones with an off-white background. Those unprofessionally photographed listings are rarely created by a brand or by Amazon, but instead by individual sellers. Such listings are less competitive than the professionally-created listings.

> **Note:** With Amazon arbitrage of any kind, you never look for profitable products to sell. Instead, you look for profitable listings to sell on.

I only needed to scroll down a couple of rows on the Amazon Gain dryer sheets before running across my first candidate:

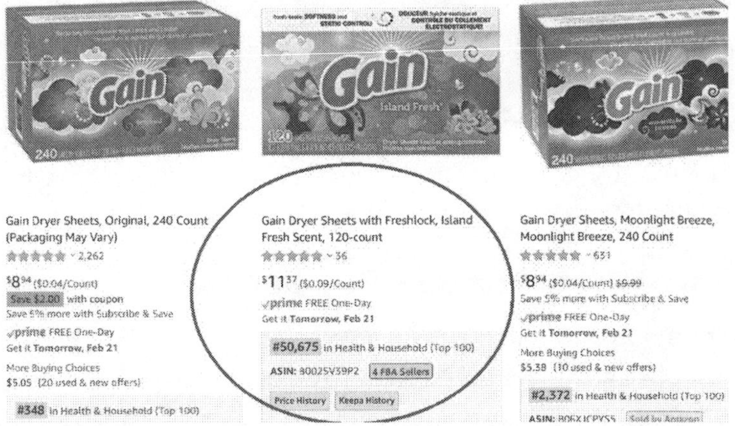

$11.57 seems high for one box of dryer sheets, but we'll only know by finding them for sale somewhere and analyzing prices and sales history. We like replens like these that aren't fragile and that don't take a lot of room to store and ship.

Where can you find these Island Fresh scented 120-count dryer sheets for sale? Copy the Amazon title and paste it into a Google search. You'll see that lots of stores carry it. When you look at the results, make sure to find the exact product you're trying to match from Amazon.

Here's one typical Google result:

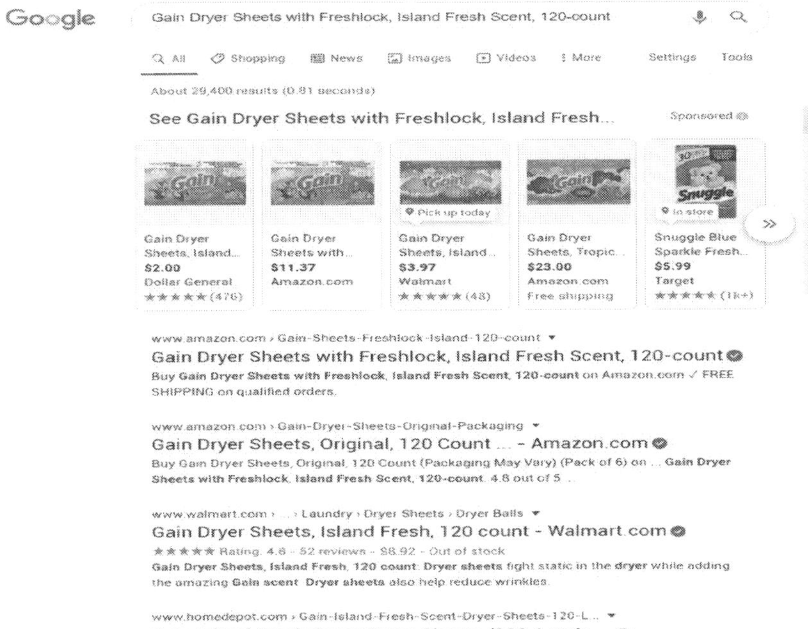

The first dryer sheet ad, Dollar General's, looks like a great candidate at $2, but clicking through to that item on DG's website shows it's only a 34-count box. We want the 120-count box.

Next, we see the very Amazon listing we used for the search.

Clicking on the next item at Walmart produces *almost* a match here:

Do you see why this won't work? The count is wrong at 105.

The remaining two sponsored ads show another Amazon listing and an incorrect match for a Snuggle item at Target.

Don't give up yet because the results below those icon-based ads could locate someone selling the Gain we want to price. A Walmart entry around the middle of the screen shows a matching box that costs nearly $9. There's no profit there. Trying further down, the Home Depot entry near the bottom sends us to this page:

You can't see the price here, but Home Depot sells these for $4.97. At an Amazon selling price of $11.37, there's almost surely not enough profit, but on smaller items like these it's not unwise to check.

Unfortunately, there's not any real profit here:

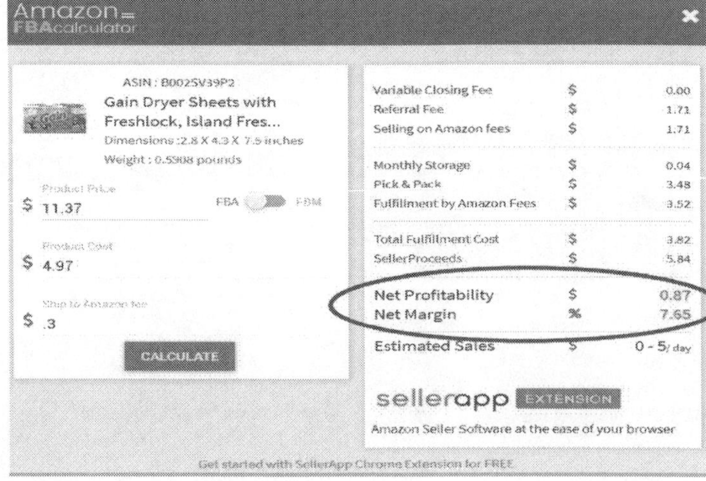

We Missed Something – Did You Catch It?

Let me review what we did with the dryer sheets:

1. I spotted the Gain dryer sheets at my house, so I did a general Amazon search for *gain dryer sheets*.
2. The goal was to locate bundles, possibly-overpriced listings, and Amazon listings with photos that indicate resellers made the listings and not the brand.
3. On Google, we found these results at the top of the sponsored listings on the search results:

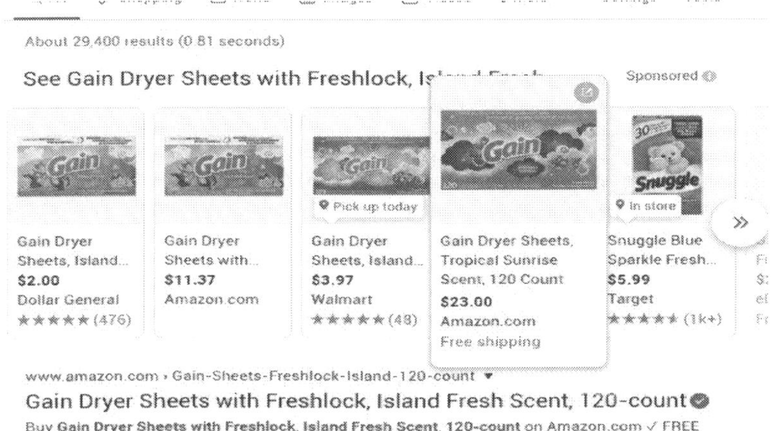

The second and fourth one represents Amazon listings. We're trying to locate places to buy them to resell on Amazon. This is why we looked at Dollar General, Walmart, and finally found the unprofitable item at Home Depot later in the search results.

But something should have caught our eye when we first reviewed this. This is the kind of thing you'll get much better at spotting. Notice I increased the size of the fourth entry in the previous image. We ran the search to locate off-Amazon dryer sheets that we could possibly resell for $11.37. But in the process, a far better Amazon listing may have appeared for us! We found a 120-count Gain dryer sheet box Amazon sells for $23.00!

Here's the Amazon page:

Everything *almost* appears to be the same box of sheets. The count is 120 but it's *Tropical Sunrise* instead of the *Island Fresh* scent. At $23 a box, more than twice what the Amazon listing sold a single box of Island Fresh for, we should search for this one instead.

If you were to do this, you'd find that Walmart retails this box for $8.94 bringing you a profit of $6.80 and an ROI of 76%! The ROI at 76% ($6.80/$8.94) more than meets the Stage One average requirement and the higher selling price helps boost your average dollar sales per item throughout your inventory.

Let's look at Keepa:

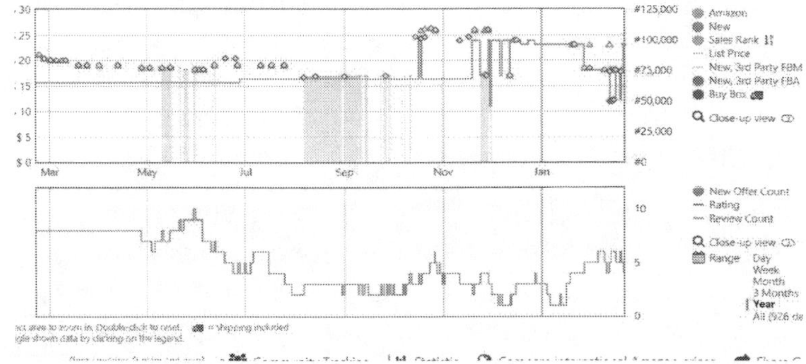

Amazon goes on and off this, but it's off enough not to worry us. The Buy Box is higher than several of the FBA sellers who hover around $18. The Buy Box is rarely as high as it happens to be right now at $23.

The number of sellers hardly ever goes over 5 and often stays from 1 to 3 – Fantastic. The rank's range from 75,000 to 100,000 is great. Keepa indicates a little risk of it dropping in price throughout the year, but the price can and does rise above $23 frequently enough.

This would be a definite replen. What a great find that was given we stumbled upon it when looking for a different scent.

The Gain Examples Are Only Models

What we saw before was a way we back into possible replens online. We'd locate a product, search Amazon for listings that caught our eyes, and then search for a place to buy them online.

I want you to get a feel for the approach. That's the only goal here.

Instead of walking down an aisle finding the next item to look for, you're coming up with items based on what you see in your home or that you see online by scrolling through a store's inventory.

Hybrid Arbitrage

This is a newer strategy that I never considered in the first edition of the book, it's something that I call Hybrid Arbitrage. The reason it's a hybrid is because it's a cross between both Retail and Online Arbitrage. Essentially, you are shopping online, but the items that are getting purchased are in your local retail stores.

It's a very basic method but one that can save you TONS of time, which is your most valuable asset. Basically, due to recent technologies and the adoption of side hustles by many people, there are services you can utilize to do your shopping for you. You can use Instacart, Shipt, DoorDash, Task Rabbit, or something similar to buy products at your local grocery store, Walmart, Target, etc. and someone that works with that service will go to the store and pick up those items for you. Typically they are delivered to you within a couple hours, at most it will be the next day.

This is an excellent way to save your time while still shopping for those replens from regional stores I mentioned earlier. Products that are unique to you, that other sellers wouldn't be able to get if they don't live in your area. Hopefully you can see the power of this Hybrid Arbitrage model as it can completely change the game for you, especially if you don't have the time or ability to go to your local store to shop and you don't want to do the regular OA model where everyone has access to the same products.

> **NOTE:** If you want to see some training on the Hybrid Arbitrage model (and many of the methods discussed in this book), you can get the free video summary, jumpstart course at askjimmysmith.com/jumpstart.

Complete Stage One!

Have you started using this book's RA and OA strategies to find replens? Let me remind you that you want to find 30 replens in the first 30 days in order to start your journey to $100,000/month.

For now, your job is to get to $10,000 in monthly replen sales in order to complete Stage One and move to Stage Two.

> **Reminder:** Don't forget to get the replen tracker to track your first 30+ replens plus all other resources from the book at askjimmysmith.com/bookresources.

Chapter 9

–

Working on Your First 30 Replens in 30 Days

Things should be coming together for you now. Here we'll review the concepts you learned in earlier chapters. I find that new replens sellers benefit from a "bird's eye view" after they've spent time learning replens sourcing.

If you have a lot of questions, this chapter might answer them. You know the basics now. Here you'll review concepts and get comfortable about what's ahead of you.

> **Note:** If you have started sourcing, that's fantastic. I assume several reading this book have. If so, you have a head start and are ahead of the game. Still, unless you've already worked on 30 replens in 30 days, even if you haven't yet fulfilled that goal, the time to start is *right now*. The exercise of finding them sets you up nicely for the rest of the travel to $100,000. You'll have far more confidence after the first 30 replens.

The roadmap I presented requires 30 replens in 30 days and you should intend on achieving that. This enables you to get the momentum you'll need and allow you to continue to grow.

> "It always seems impossible until it's done."
> ~Nelson Mandela

In Review

At this point, it'll help focus you by reviewing a few key points.

Don't Scan Barcodes

Don't scan UPC barcodes to find product listings as you walk down aisles. It's tempting because it's so easy. The reason it's a bad way to find profitable listings to sell on is precisely because it's easy. Most people start RA by scanning barcodes and many stick with that as their primary method. They find fewer profitable listings to sell on which makes the listings they do find more competitive than others might be.

> **Note:** Scanning barcodes on tags actually works best for sourcing shoes & clothing. These don't work as well for replens as other product categories however because of the constantly changing seasons and styles.

To those who still scan UPC codes, it's a numbers game. They scan, scan, scan, moving quickly from product to product. Eventually, one will be profitable. (Far fewer will be profitable than *you'll* find.) Many who begin scanning don't stick with RA long because they tire of leaving the store often with nothing to resell.

Use Picture Searching If You Like That

Instead of scanning UPC codes, you know you can use the Amazon Seller App's camera to point at a product and attempt to match it with an Amazon product page.

The picture search is surprisingly accurate – unless it's not and then it can find horrible matches that seem to have nothing to do with the item you're in front of. The primary drawback is its lack of speed. It can take the camera a while to focus on the product. Once the camera focuses, it can take the app a few seconds of interaction with Amazon's servers to find or reject the image.

When you can't find many listings by typing, the picture scan can find more matching listings. Don't use the picture search most of the time, but it's a decent backup when you're not getting quite as many results as you expect.

> **Tip:** Amazon's Buyer app can produce a different set of search results than any of the seller apps including Amazon's. When you can't seem to locate as many listings as you think you should, type the item into Amazon's Buyer app and see what comes up.

Typing Your Search Produces the Best Results

Typing a general search phrase for what you want to evaluate is the tried and true way to find replens reliably. The reason is that all Amazon's search engines are buyer-centric. Amazon cares far more about what buyers type than what you type. Amazon wants buyers to find what they're looking for.

When a buyer searches for a *red 3-ring binder*, Amazon wants as many listings with red 3-ring binders to appear that the buyer can scroll through.

That's why a typed search phrase is always king for Amazon searches. Nearly 100% of every search my team performs in stores is typed.

> **Tip:** If you know how to use your cell phone's voice-to-text feature, speak the search phrase instead of typing it. Depending on how clearly you speak, how fast your phone is, and how much noise is around you, speaking is as fast or faster than typing your search phrase.

Take Your Time

As you go through products in an aisle you're currently in, traverse methodically and slowly. I can spend hours in one aisle. I don't want to rush things, or I'll miss the only reason I'm there: to find profitable replens.

Slow and steady wins the race.

Methodically go through every item in the aisle, typing each in. Along the way, you'll reverse search and you may find bundles of closely-related products in your searches by being general. When we first started, I didn't do general searches. I thought I could decide what to skip because I knew that certain things "couldn't be good." Brittany would come behind me and look up ones I skipped; they'd invariably be a replen!

> **Tip:** When you walk through all items in a section, you likely will find more than one replen. Not only that, being so close together makes them super-simple to buy each month afterwards.

You might determine that an entire brand is bad for you to source, perhaps due to major gating issues or the weight and costs aren't going to make the items profitable. In such cases, you can go ahead and skip those items.

Want Some Encouragement?

Perhaps this will inspire you.

I've spent from 30 minutes to as many as *four hours* on one side of one aisle hunting for replens. The time it can take happens because I don't skip items. In addition, the more successful I am in a section, the slower I go.

When I start finding multiple replens in the same section, I usually *keep* finding them. I go slow because I don't want to miss others that might be close by. The four hours I once spent on one side of an aisle resulted in between 30 and 40 replens before I moved to the next aisle.

30 to 40 replens in four hours! That's more than half the 67 replens required to reach Stage Two.

When you look at it that way, four hours isn't long at all. Especially when you realize 30 to 40 replens results in about $5,000/month in sales over and over if you meet the averages discussed at the beginning of the book.

Generally, you'll take longer to achieve the same success in an aisle than I can do in an hour *but you're just starting out.* I was at your level when we started. It won't be long before you can match what we do. Therefore, know now that you're likely to take more than an hour in every aisle, maybe two hours, maybe three or more. Knowing that enables you to get comfortable being somewhat uncomfortable.

> **Note:** Is there *really* anything uncomfortable about finding money that's going to keep coming your way month after month, year after year?

Once you finish an aisle, go to the *next* aisle. Don't jump around stores going from category to category. That kind of hunting doesn't keep you focused. You'll lose the methodical mindset you'll need to find quality replens. Also, you'll likely miss bundles that could contain some things where you are and the rest of the bundles on the next aisle if the product line extends that far.

Make it Boring

Especially starting out, go at a snail's pace. Be boring. You're not doing this for excitement now. Trust me when I tell you that as you begin to find replens, it gets less boring. Your confidence builds, you find more replens because of the confidence, you go slightly faster only because you learn to check Keepa faster, and you'll enter a smooth groove before you know it. Listen to music or your favorite podcast if that helps keep you focused & interested in this process.

Start general and get specific.

First type *pepsodent toothpaste* when you get to the first Pepsodent Toothpaste in your aisle.

> **Note:** Think about why scanning barcodes is the worst method. Scanning a barcode is the *most* specific search you could request. You're telling Amazon this: "Only one item on earth has this UPC code and I want to find the one listing that this one, specific product sells on."

Barcodes violate our general-to-specific policy.

The more general your search, the more listings with Pepsodent Toothpaste appear. You'll also see more bundles and multipacks.

As you scroll through general search results, you'll begin to notice unusual listings that sell for higher-than-expected prices. Also, you'll notice that perhaps cinnamon-flavored Pepsodent Toothpaste sells at higher prices than other Pepsodents in front of you. You may never have noticed that if you'd scanned or typed a more specific phrase such as, *peppermint pepsodent mint flavor toothpaste 5 ounces*.

Yes, when you finally get to cinnamon-flavored Pepsodent in the aisle, you might have noticed the Amazon prices are higher, but consider this: What if the store you're in doesn't sell cinnamon-flavored Pepsodent? You'd never know cinnamon might offer better profits had you not typed the general search phrase. Now, you have new knowledge. When you get home, you use the OA tactics from the last chapter to find who sells cinnamon-flavored Pepsodent toothpaste in your town, or perhaps at a good price online.

> **Tip:** By starting general when you get to a new set of products in a new section or new aisle, you'll once in a while find that an entire brand is dead on Amazon. You might find everything's gated for you there. Perhaps Amazon's on every listing and protects its own Buy Box too dearly. The general search might save you from a lot of wasted item-by-item searching these rare times.

After searching for a general phrase or two, add keywords such as *bundle, variety pack,* and *set* to your searches. Here, you're sort of thinking more like a seller than a buyer because buyers don't generally add "bundle" to their searches. Still, remember that bundled listings often offer higher profits. The majority of our replen inventory consists of bundled items. By adding those keywords, you get more options to sell.

Later, get specific and try to find each and every item you see in front of you. Some listings actually appear that never appeared in the general search.

> **Note:** If one or more of your replens are meltable items, such as Hersheys chocolate bars, they aren't replens 12 months a year. Amazon doesn't allow meltable items in FBA warehouses from May through mid-October because of hot weather. If you find meltable replens, you'll adjust your average numbers for selling them only 6 or 7 months each year. An alternative is to sell them as Merchant Fulfilled items year-round and insert cold packs in the packages you ship to buyers (available at Uline.com).

Are Other Sellers MF or FBA?

If Keepa shows lots of sellers on a profitable item, check to see how many sellers are FBA and how many are MF. We'll often find things sold only by Merchant Fulfilled sellers. If the product sells well enough to test, we gladly test a few because we'll end up being the only FBA seller on the listing.

FBA sellers generally get more sales than MF sellers. FBA sellers often own the Buy Box. Most Amazon buyers have Amazon Prime accounts and they prefer to buy from FBA sellers (even though most won't know what FBA means) because FBA items always offer free shipping.

We generally start 10% higher than the last few MF sales due to the fact that FBA commands higher prices.

The Last Step?

ACK!

You've *not* found a replen until you check Keepa.

> **Tip:** You have quick access to an item's Keepa chart from within the Scoutify app (free with an InventoryLab subscription) or any other sourcing app. If you use only the Amazon Seller app to source, you'll have to keep your phone's web browser open to check Keepa.com and copy ASINs from the Seller app to the website for each item you check. Keepa does have a way to speed up searches by using Facebook Messenger. If you use the mobile version

of Firefox, a Keepa extension is available that could make finding charts slightly easier on phones. Additionally, Keepa does have it's own app for checking these charts but I typically just use the browser on my phone as it is connected to Scoutify and other sourcing apps.

Don't Stop

With the help of this book, you're likely to find more replens than scheduled over the next few weeks and months. If you find 50 the first 30 days, for instance, don't stop! Keep grinding away towards that $100,000 goal.

I designed each stage after the four general stages our business took to reach $100,000 per month. We shortened the path some by hiring help a little earlier than we suggest in future chapters. Your situation is certainly different from ours. If you can hire help far earlier than we did you'll far more quickly reach $100,000 in monthly sales. In doing that, you have far more costs earlier than those who stick to the four stages' exact suggested schedule.

Another way to grow faster even if you don't have enough capital to hire help earlier is to find far more replens earlier than the 4-stage plan requires.

In Stage One, if you find the required 67 replens in the first month, you're ready to go to Stage Two. Continue that pace and you'll hit Stage Three fast too. Even if you don't want to implement all of Stage three yet, keep finding more and more replens earlier than you'd planned. Don't stop at 67 if you find those relatively quickly.

> **Warning:** I've described a few product situations where I suggested caution and to only source two to four items the first month as a test. Depending on how many of these you find, certainly source those, but you'll need more than 67 replens to hit $10,000. The math for $10,000 assumes you have 67 products that each sell *an average* of about 10 every month. The good news is you'll find replens that sell more than 10 each month. When you do, your average sales

per item goes up without you adding extra replens to make up for slower sellers.

Adjust Down When Needed

If your finances are limited when you start, you might have to take longer to move from Stage One to Stage Two. That's fine.

Perhaps you can't afford 67 replens as quickly as two and a half months. Hitting each stage is more about replen levels than timeframes. If you take an extra month or two or three to get your first few replens turning over to provide capital you need to grow the rest, take that time.

If you get great at finding replens early, but your capital or time is limited, consider tightening your parameters and require that all replens have a 100% minimum ROI. Your returned capital will be far larger than it otherwise would be, and you'll then afford to increase the number of replens.

You Might Not Like One or More Replens You Find

You'll recall that 5% or so of replens drop off each month. Therefore, you'll need to add about 5% of last month's replen count to make up for the loss.

Drop-offs don't always happen because the price tanks or Amazon gates an item. You might source a certain replen one month only to find that it's a heavier item than you expected and adds an extra dollar to ship it to the FBA warehouses.

In addition, some items take far too long to prep than they're worth.

For these and more reasons, don't feel obligated to keep a replen you don't want to source again. Obviously, your replen count drops when you remove it, but that's fine; add an extra replen next month to make up for the loss.

Part 3
–
Stage Two: From $10,000 to $40,000

Chapter 10
–
Stage Two: Moving from $10,000 to $40,000 in Replens

"I have not failed. I've just found 10,000 ways that won't work."
~Thomas A. Edison

Unlike Thomas Edison, you found 10,000 ways that *do* work in the form of sales!

Reaching $10,000 in sales, you deserve a hearty congratulations! Many thousands of people have sold on Amazon but never reached that level. You're in an elite group.

But stay awake, you're not even close to stopping now. You didn't come this far to relax yet. Plus, if you actually went from $0 to $10,000 in replens, I have no doubt that you're extremely motivated to increase that income… and you can.

This stage shows you exactly how to do it.

> **Note:** If you're still on Stage One but want to read ahead here to get of glimpse of what's next, *great!* Knowing what's in store always helps. Know, however, you don't need to study this part of the book until you're at the end of Stage One. One thing I don't want to happen is to let this stage discourage you if you're not yet here. When you reach $10,000 in sales, you'll be absolutely ready for all we discuss here.

Stage Two's Mindset

Whereas Stage One is a learning stage, Stage Two is a honing stage. You'll improve your skills and hunt for lots of replens.

I call this second stage, "The Grinding Stage."

> "A dream doesn't become reality through magic; it takes sweat, determination and hard work."
> ~ Colin Powell

Mindset is everything.

Your mindset enables you to focus on the end goal: scaling your now-successful replen business to achieve the next peak of $40,000.

Both mindset and work ethic must be rock solid to accomplish Stage Two. You won't necessarily work four times harder than you did in Stage One, but you will work harder to reach Stage Two's $40,000 goal. You'll find far more replens and you're still shopping for Stage One replens while looking for new ones. Here, you'll not only continue working *in* your business, but you will begin the all-important work *on* your business. As you get closer to $40,000, you'll have some systems in place or be in the process of finalizing them to handle the larger business that comes next.

Here in Stage Two, many factors appear that affect your effort levels and add new challenges. Fortunately, many of the new factors you begin seeing in Stage Two are good.

You now have confidence you didn't have the first few weeks of finding replens. This greatly speeds up your finds. From all your work in Stage One, you'll almost now have a sort of "sixth sense" where you more quickly rule in or rule out replen candidates without laboring over *all* the analysis and calculations you may have done previously.

> **Note:** Once you hit Stage One's $10,000 sales level, it may help not to immediately focus on the $40,000. That is quite

a stretch from where you are. Focus mostly on $10,000 increments to get there, one at a time, three more to go. Focus on $20,000. Then $30,000. Then $40,000. Doing this enables you to stay real and not talk yourself into an "I can't possibly hit $40k!" negative mindset. ***Focus on what you can control which is finding more replens, the sales and profits will naturally come from that.***

Cashflow is King

In Stage Two, it's even more vital to maintain your average selling price, average ROI, and sales velocity. At this level, your capital can easily drop if you don't maintain eagle eyes on your numbers. In a page or two, you'll see the Stage Two numbers you require. Those are critical to keep unless you have plenty of outside capital available. If you drop below this stage's required average ROI on a few items, you'll need to locate enough that return far higher than your ROI requirements to keep your averages in line.

> **Note:** Believe it or not, Stage Three and Stage Four are somewhat easier on you than the first two are. (They were for us.) Stage One is the slow, non-confident learning stage. Stage Two is the grinding stage. As you get closer to Stage Two's goal of $40,000 per month, new opportunities open with that level of capital that weren't possible before. You'll leverage the extra capital to reduce your time and effort as you enter Stage Three.

One of the primary reasons to grind it out in Stage Two is to build enough capital to invest in a shopper or a prepper and shipper. Once you hit $40,000 you can easily use some capital to hire prepping and shipping help instead of pouring 100% of the capital back into inventory.

Brittany and I reached the end of Stage Two at $25,000 and not $40,000. By the time we hit $25,000 in sales, we realized that lots of factors worked together to make more growth impossible for us without getting help. This is why our Stage Three started earlier than it may for you. If you can grind Stage Two all the way to $40,000 with just you (and any immediate family members who may help), then you'll be better leveraged to begin implementing Stage Three's tactics of growth. If, however, Stage Two becomes too much of a Goliath to tackle before $40,000 and your business gets to the point of, "we quit or we get help," move early to Stage Three.

> **Note:** If you can't afford to shorten Stage Two but still need help, you'll have to stop using 100% your capital for inventory or bring more in from elsewhere (personal saving, small loan, or whatever). Or, go slower than Stage Two typically takes. Perhaps you'll add new replens more slowly so you can get all the shopping, prepping, and shipping done – especially if you're doing everything yourself. You might need to raise the average ROI or sales prices of new replens to build capital faster (making the number of new replens you find *slightly* harder). Each stage's dollar ranges in this book are optimal if you can adhere to them. Try to reach each stage's top dollar goal before starting the next stage's strategies. If you need to change sooner, great! Just know you'll have tradeoffs either in needing a little outside capital from your savings or loans, or you'll need to go slower than you otherwise would.

Stage Two Tools

You still need at least one seller app and you already have that, the Amazon seller app. In addition, you won't be getting rid of Keepa any time soon (probably never!).

Now that you're above $10,000 per month, it's helpful to get a second seller app if you haven't already.

> **Note:** If you primarily do Online Arbitrage, plenty of online tools and helpful Amazon Chrome extensions are available so that you don't necessarily need any other cell phone based sourcing app besides the Amazon Seller app. Head over to askjimmysmith.com/best-resources to see my most up-to-date list of suggestions.

This additional seller app gives you far quicker access to Keepa than you can get with a phone's Amazon Seller app and the Keepa.com web page alone. You'll view Keepa charts *far* faster this way.

> **Tip:** If you already have a subscription to InventoryLab to help with accounting and shipping, Scoutify comes free with InventoryLab and it's also a great app that gives quick access to Keepa charts.

You'll always keep the Amazon Seller app installed. No sourcing app can do a picture search like it. Also, Amazon's app gives you access to many areas of your Amazon account.

Another benefit of Scoutify or another sourcing app is their Buy List functionality. This greatly speeds up your FBA shipments. I'll cover this in more detail later, but as you shop and find a new replen, you *right there in the store* will save the item, quantity, cost, the listing you'll list the replen on, where you purchased the item, and more. Entering this information right in the store as you put a newly-sourced item in your cart is tremendously simpler and faster than entering your purchased inventory later when you get home.

You best know which listing you want to sell an item on *right there in the store when you decide a listing is profitable enough to sell on.* By the time you get home, this is the common lament: "Now which of the 23,000 Hershey Candy listings did I want to sell this candy bar on again?"

The Buy List is most helpful if you subscribe to and use InventoryLab (found at InventoryLab.com). It's difficult to keep track of an Amazon business by the time you get to the end of Stage One without InventoryLab. Therefore, if you're not yet subscribing to InventoryLab, you need to do so immediately. The cost is about $50 per month.

Replen Management

Managing replens is more important in Stage Two. Monthly, you'll be buying, restocking, and shipping more and more items. You don't want to overship items that still have plenty of inventory in stock and you don't want too many items to sell out before you're able to get replacements sent.

In Stage One and even some of Stage Two, you can manage your replen inventory and restocks easily without a formal system other than a notebook or electronic worksheet. Stage Three gets you to a point where everything becomes unwieldy if you don't have a good system in place to monitor inventory levels, shipments, and so on. To help with Stage Three, you need to implement a replens management system sometime in Stage Two.

Remember: Stage Two is the time to implement a replens management system *because* your replen levels are still manageable as opposed to what they'll be when you get to $40,000 in sales.

It is now that you want to institute a formal replen management system. That system might be a blank notebook with columns and lines to track inventory. You can find this in an office supply store. The system might be an Excel or Google Sheets electronic worksheet. To maximize your replens management and minimize your time to monitor things, you might see the benefit of using a software system designed specifically for the way you work. Any of those systems can be an inventory-helper, a time-saver, and a money-maker once you hit Stage Three.

Whatever you decide to use, implement that system in Stage Two. Plan for growth, you're still not close to even halfway to your $100,000 goal. (You'll get halfway before you know it!) When starting, the thought of moving to Stage Three with a target of $70,000 in monthly sales might seem impossible. Until now, I bet you couldn't imagine selling $10,000 every month, right? And $40,000 is directly in sight.

You won't handle Stage Three without some sort of replen management system. I'll help you put one in place.

Stage Two's Math

Maintain your $15 ASP (Average Selling Price) and 10 sales per month per replen average.

With that average price, you'll need about 2,667 sales each month to reach Stage Two's $40,000. With 10 of each replen selling monthly, you'll increase your number of replens to 267 (2,667 / 10). That's when you hit $40,000.

> **Note:** If you're starting Stage One but reading ahead, super! Don't obsess on *these* numbers. Stage One's numbers and strategies should be your only focus.

Stage Two takes about 10 months to get to $40,000. This assumes you're finding 30 new replens each month. Adjust that time depending on how profitable your finds are in Stage Two and how many of Stage One's replens do or don't drop off. About 5% of our replens drop off monthly and need replacing. Although in some cases it can go up to 10%, especially if there are any supply chain issues going on in your area or with your store. If you also see a higher than 5% drop-off rate, your $40,000 goal might take as long as a year or more to achieve since you'll have to make up for those drop-offs by replacing them. Also, if you find more than 30 per month, then you can get to $40,000/month much faster!

Along the way, take account of your own success finding replens. If you can comfortably raise your ASP to $20 and find an average of 30 each month, you'll hit $40,000 faster than estimated here. You can speed up Stage Two's time by raising your average number of sales per item to about 15 each month if you search harder for those better-selling replens.

End Stage Two at $25,000 to $40,000

As I mentioned, we ended Stage Two and jumped to the Stage Three strategy at $25,000. First, we didn't know what a stage was because we were living through what I'm teaching you here. We had struggles you'll avoid because I'll warn you about them and explain how to avoid them. Only looking back were we able to systematize a $0 to $100,000 monthly replens strategy for you.

If you choose to end Stage Two before you hit $40,000 because you can't handle the shopping, prepping and shipping, and managing replens by yourself, your only problem might be capital as you first move up to Stage Three's strategy. Slow down if you must. Getting to Stage Three slowly won't be a roadblock to your success.

Still, the reality is *if* you can move to Stage Three somewhat earlier, as we did, your success speeds up as your capital holds.

Using a Replens Goals Sheet

I've created a worksheet that'll be handy here at the start of Stage Two. This worksheet enables you to adjust your numbers – your average selling price or total number of replens or average number of sales of each replen per month – and see how this affects your timing at each stage's goal.

Remember, to get all of the resources for this book including this goals sheet, go to: askjimmysmith.com/bookresources

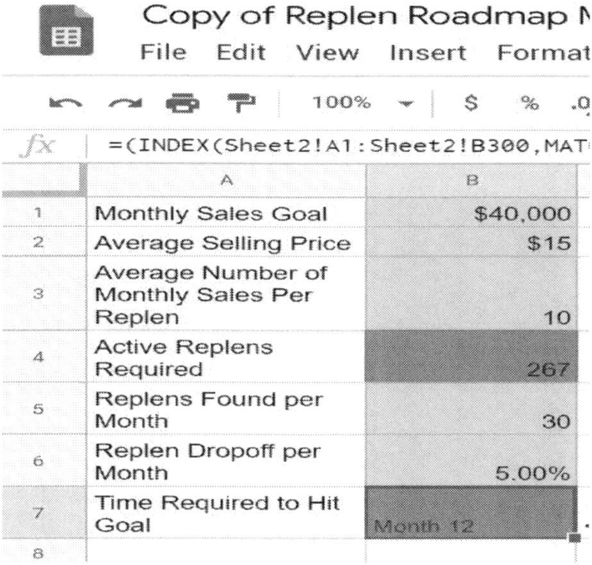

Copy of Replen Roadmap N

File Edit View Insert Format

100% $ % .0

fx =(INDEX(Sheet2!A1:Sheet2!B300,MAT

	A	B
1	Monthly Sales Goal	$40,000
2	Average Selling Price	$15
3	Average Number of Monthly Sales Per Replen	10
4	Active Replens Required	267
5	Replens Found per Month	30
6	Replen Dropoff per Month	5.00%
7	Time Required to Hit Goal	Month 12
8		

You see that you'll reach $40,000 in the twelfth month. It takes you about 10 months to reach your Stage Two's goal, but the worksheet shows 12 months because Stage One's 67 products took you just over a couple of months at 30 replens every 30 days.

What if you were stricter with your requirements and sourced only replens that averaged a $20 selling price instead of $15? You can adjust the ASP in the worksheet to learn your $40,000 goal only takes 8 months, plus you'll need fewer replens (200) to achieve $40,000 shown here:

Copy of Replen Roadmap Math

File Edit View Insert Format Da

100% $ % .0 .00

10

A	B	
Monthly Sales Goal	$40,000	
Average Selling Price	$20	
Average Number of Monthly Sales Per Replen	10	
Active Replens Required	200	
Replens Found per Month	30	
Replen Dropoff per Month	5.00%	
Time Required to Hit Goal	Month 8	<<<<--

Note: You can adjust any yellow cell to change the bottom-line time required to accomplish a goal including the monthly drop-off percentage if you're seeing that be an issue in your area & business.

Faster Shipments

Often, Amazon sellers aren't as quick and efficient as they can be, both in sourcing as well as managing inventory. Even shipping your replens can be greatly sped up. Since you probably don't have employees during most or all of Stage Two, you may not be thinking ahead about your shipping process.

It's time to standardize and speed up your shipping process.

The prep and ship process becomes fairly rote with replens. The second time you prep and ship a replen is simple because you've prepped and shipped it once before. As you get more and more replens, you start to forget the best way you found to prep and ship each one.

As I mentioned earlier in this chapter, Scoutify or any other sourcing app works to speed your shipping process when you add to a Buy List as you find a new replen or shop for an existing one. You upload the Buy List from your phone to InventoryLab, populating the inventory that you're about to prep and ship next. This enables you to start the prep and ship process far faster and get shipments sent into FBA quicker.

> **Note:** Every day that you have unsent inventory costs you money. Prices can easily change the longer you wait as others find and send in the same items. Your money is tied up when the inventory sits in your house or warehouse. It cannot sell there. Stage One and Stage Two can be capital drains if you had little to start with so *get inventory sent quickly*. You want and need to churn profits fast so you can buy the next larger batch.

One way to help track things better in InventoryLab (or possibly in any of its competitors such as Boxt – which works in international marketplaces as well as the US) is to create merchant SKUs called *MSKUs*. These will be your own identification system for your products. Buyers never see the MSKU with FBA. MSKUs exist to let you track any information for each item you sell. Not every seller needs to use MSKUs, but we find them extremely helpful with replens.

Here's a sample pattern you can use:

Date-Number-Store-Cost

For example: 122820-1-WALMART-4.97

Again, the MSKU is yours to use for whatever product-level information you want to track. No two MSKUs can be the same so just in case we buy two items on December 28, 2020 for $4.97 at Walmart, the *Number* lets us make those MSKUs unique from each other.

If you have both replen and non-replen inventory, as most will, it helps to preface your replen MSKUs with the word *REPLEN* or *REP* like this:

REPLEN-Date-Number-Store-Cost

Rarely will every item in your inventory be a replen so the *REPLEN* prefix lets you to quickly find all the replens in a batch of inventory.

For example: REPLEN-122820-2-WALMART-4.97

You will either need to add these to your Buy List before uploading or Inventory Lab can auto-generate these for you using a custom formula.

Our RA Shipment Process

For OA, once items arrive from your source, the prep and ship procedure is identical to RA except you usually don't have to remove retail price stickers. Some resellers who buy inventory online use a prep and ship center. In that case, they have online sites ship all their inventory to the prep center who then preps and ships the items to FBA. We suggest checking out prepcenternetwork.com to see a list of vetted prep centers if you need one.

We primarily do RA and the odds are good you do also. Stage Two is the time when you want to take a good look at your process because prepping and shipping becomes a bottleneck in this business very quickly. We're going to discuss a high-level overview of our workflow that you should consider imitating.

> **Note:** A little later, Stage Three's replen levels will require even more discussion on your prep and ship workflow because you'll bring one or more employees into the mix by then.

Here's the general prep and ship process that should work for most of you with just about any sourcing app:

1. Email your Buy Lists to yourself from your phone.
2. Open the Buy List and add MSKUs to that Buy List. You must add your MSKUs beforehand because when you upload your Buy List to your prep/ship software, it automatically adds generic MSKUs if none are present.

3. Upload the Buy List to InventoryLab or whatever shipping software you use.
4. Print all your FNSKU stickers you'll apply to your items.
5. Prep and ship the merchandise to FBA.

> **Note:** If you are using Scoutify with InventoryLab, the Buy List is automatically available within InventoryLab in the Prep/Ship section of the website without the need to email it to yourself. Also, with InventoryLab, you can have it create custom MSKUs for you within their software so you don't have to add them before uploading a Buy List. It's a super simple procedure and easily found in the help section of their website.

The most important advice I can give you at this time is this: document the process for future employees. Begin doing this early in Stage Two when you have fewer items to prep and ship and have extra time to document the process than you'll ever have moving forward.

> **Note:** If you use a prep center for OA items, document what you do for that process as well, even though you perform fewer tasks than when you prep yourself. Again, *this* is the time to document your process.

> **Tip:** Use your cell phone to create short videos for different stages of your prep and ship routine if you find that easier than describing each detail in a document. A screen recorder such as Loom can capture your screen in videos and you can narrate over the recording as you record what you're doing.

We prefer screen shots and written instructions over videos or screen-recording software. If you use videos, the delivery can become a problem when training people later. Not every part of the process can be recorded. You'll need to write about several steps throughout the process as well as use videos. How do you create a training package that ensures your future employees will read the correct order of documentation and watch the correct videos in the order needed?

Certainly, you can create such training that combines written and recorded instructions, but we find that saving screen shots and placing them throughout our written instructions is a far simpler method to produce and for new employees to follow. Printed documentation with screenshots conveys all the training we need to give.

> **Tip:** If you do use videos, you can hire a Virtual Assistant to write out the written instructions for you by transcribing the videos and have them take screenshots from the video to place in the document for picture references. This might cost a little bit of money but it will save you TONS of time vs writing out the procedures yourself.

Things will change in your process. Features of your software will change. If you've created a video-based course, you'll be re-shooting videos to reflect those changes in the process. Changing a screen shot or two, along with the text description of that part of the process, is far easier to keep your documentation up to date as changes happen.

Keep all your instructions in Google Docs for easy sharing.

> **Note:** Microsoft Word users can use shared Dropbox folders if you prefer Word over Docs. We find Google Docs easier because not everybody has Microsoft products and no matter where your employee wants to read the training instructions, they'll be able to read them in Docs without first opening Word on their laptop or phone. You can use Word to create your documents if you prefer Word's tools and upload them to Google Docs for your staff to train with.

30 minutes of documentation now saves *hours* of time later.

To get our list of resources, including our supplies list that we use in our business, go here: askjimmysmith.com/bookresources

When Do You Outsource?

When do you begin to offload repeatable tasks such as prepping and shipping?

If you follow the $0 to $100,000 plan to the letter, you will get help with your business in Stage Three. Moving past Stage Two's $40,000 sales is extremely difficult to do without help. You simply won't be able to prep, ship, buy existing replens, and find new replens at that level without stretching yourself so thin you might reach a breaking point where you begin to slack off, give up, make mistakes, and harm all the work you did before. However, $40,000 is the upper limit for this stage because I know sellers that reached this level with no help before they started outsourcing more.

This book is designed for you to hire in Stage Three at $40,000 in sales. That's great if you can wait that long. You'll have more capital to invest in Stage Two inventory if you don't spend money on an employee.

Still, from $25,000 to $40,000, doing all the work yourself becomes a chore. A *big* chore.

> "Only do what only you can do in your business."
> ~ Jim Cockrum, *Silent Sales Machine*

Brittany and I worked our business together but even with the two of us, when we reached $25,000 in sales, we needed help. We weren't growing to the level we thought we could grow by ourselves. As I said in the Introduction, our tremendous growth occurred only *after* we got help.

There's no assurance the same phenomenon will happen for you, but hired help enables you to get out of your own way (prepping and shipping, the more mundane and trainable aspect of a replens business) so that you can focus on what you do well by now: finding new replens.

> **Tip:** If you see the need for help before Stage Three but hiring help right now during Stage Two seems too much of

a capital drain, consider tightening your sourcing parameters to increase your average item sales price and the ROI you require. This will increase your capital faster and enables you to hire sooner. Doing so might slow down the speed at which you find replens, but the ones you find will be more profitable.

Here's the bottom line: hire help as soon as you can afford to do so. If you can do so in Stage Two, do it.

The reason I made the Stage Two's range go from $10,000 to $40,000 is that I know people who waited until they hit $40,000 in monthly sales before they hired help. I know it's possible to do that and for a few it's a must because of capital constraints or the fact immediate family members could take some of the load off here and there.

I definitely would have shortened Stage Two for the book had I not seen others wait until $40,000. I would have made Stage Two's range go from $10,000 to $25,000 because one of the highlights of Stage Three is the hiring process as you'll see when we get to our Stage Three coverage.

The thought of outsourcing to somebody might seem like the largest pain of the business. Consider the benefits. Your time is freed up, if for nothing else then for spending time with friends and family that's possibly been lacking the past few months in Stage One and growing into Stage Two. You'll have more time to find replens and therefore find them faster, increasing your capital, and decreasing the time you reach Stage Three.

What Can You Outsource?

For most people, this is the order of tasks you will outsource:

- Prep and ship
- Buying existing replens
- Shopping for new replens

If you're not quite ready to hire help for any of these items, consider hiring a VA (*Virtual Assistant*) to help with account management and maintenance and to deal with returns and getting reimbursed for Amazon issues. You can locate VAs that will follow your return requirements and use OA to locate online replens. A typical VA for those tasks cost from $3 to $5 per hour. Finally, a VA can help you with replen management.

> **Note:** I speak more about hiring employees in chapters 12 and 13. I included hiring information about VAs there because it fits in better with the overall theme of hiring helpers overall. Anytime you think a VA might benefit you, even if that is long before you reach Stage Four where I discuss the VA hiring process, you can always jump ahead to Chapter 13 and utilize the information for finding good VAs, including the best places for you to find trusted and vetted VAs.

I did do a course with Ryan Reger and Honey Woods on Outsourcing if you're looking for more information regarding that specifically. You can check it out at askjimmysmith.com/sell-on-amazon.

Replen Management

In my private Facebook group for my course, *$0 to $100,000 in Replens*, the questions I get asked mostly concern replen management. How does one track replens? How many of each existing replen do I replenish this month? How many dropped off for whatever reason? How many do I need to source new this month? And so on.

At the end of Stage One, you'll no doubt begin to see the need for replen management. Before you reach the end of Stage Two, you'll *require* some sort of system to manage your replens properly.

> **Do What I Say, Not What I Did**
>
> I'm embarrassed to admit that Brittany and I had nothing, *no replen management system of any kind*, until we hit $75,000 in sales per month, in Stage 4.

> We had no software, no worksheet, not even a notebook with written notes in it to manage our giant list of replens.
>
> Trust me, we *strongly* wish we had something earlier.

Without any kind of system, here's what we did and what you'll have to do:

> In the store, we used the Amazon Seller app to check inventory to see if we needed to replenish an item. We'd walk up and down the aisles checking, "Do we need more of this toothpaste?" We'd look through inventory for the next item in the aisle we happened to be in and looked to see if that needed replenishing while we were there, and so on. Back at home, when we had a chance, we'd scroll through inventory and see what out of stock items needed to be sent in. If we had any of that item at home, we'd send it in. Otherwise, we'd write down what we needed to repurchase to send in and buy it on our next shopping trip.

We'd lose track of things. There's no other possible outcome. When nothing is systematized, important details slip through the cracks. You'll start to miss out-of-stock items and not replenish them as soon as you should. You'll go off the $0 to $100,000 track and wonder why your numbers aren't quite what they should be.

My suggestion for now is to make a list of the replens you have in your business. Here are the items you must track for each item in your inventory:

- SKU
- ASIN
- Amazon Link
- Product Title
- OA Link for Repurchase (if necessary)
- Cost

- Sell Price
- Profit
- Sales per month
- Inventory Level

These details are important to know when to replenish, how many to replenish, and is it worth replenishing again. A system also helps you start the process with future VAs or employees.

A VA can manage this list for you. I strongly suggest that once you reach 100 or more SKUs, you hire a VA to manage this list once or twice a week. Your time is worth far more than the $5 per hour that a VA will cost you.

Here is a Replen Management Sheet for You

We created a Replen Management Sheet for people in our Facebook group and for you to use. While it's not nearly as robust as our Replen Management Software (replendashboard.com), you'll find that this worksheet gets you through the middle stages of your journey well.

Remember, go here to download a copy of your worksheet and the rest of the resources for this book: askjimmysmith.com/bookresources

Click to copy the sheet and then it'll be your own sheet that you can make changes to and use without others seeing it. After clicking to make a copy, you also can download it to your computer to manage it with Excel. However, using Google Sheets enables your VAs and other employees to access the sheet easily.

Here's what it looks like when you first open the Replen Management Sheet:

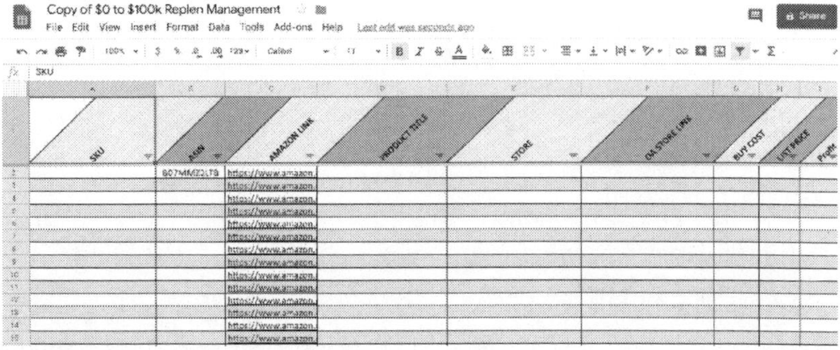

When you first use the worksheet, enter any replens you already have in your inventory. As you find new replens, you'll add those to the worksheet in new rows.

First, you enter the SKU (your MSKU) and then the ASIN. The Amazon Link automatically updates on that row to become a hyperlink you can click to jump to that item on Amazon.

The title is nice to keep because you might source similar items and the title lets you know the difference between them, such as a 2-pack, 3-pack, and 6-pack. The store (or OA store link) where you found the replen is needed so you can replenish it when it's time to do so.

The Cost field tracks costs that were profitable. If an item increases in price, you should check the numbers to make sure the item falls into your required profitability returns. If not, consider this a replen drop-off item and return any inventory you haven't yet sent to FBA back to the store.

Your list price will be what you first listed the item for (the Buy Box at the time). If the list price changes, you (or preferably your VA) will update the list price with the new one to determine if the profit numbers to the right of the List Price are still in your range.

> **Note:** Don't let the errors running down the ROI field worry you. The ROI calculation produces an error code, **#DIV/0!** (division by zero is mathematically impossible) when you don't have a Profit or Cost entered. As you populate the worksheet with new values, the ROI error

disappears and the correct, calculated ROI% fills the cell as shown next.

The final three columns are what your VA can help with the most: In Stock, Sales Last 30 Days (Units), and Buy Amount. The Buy Amount is a calculated field that updates as soon as the In Stock and the Sales Last 30 Days (Units) fields are entered. If, for instance, you have 15 in stock but sold 30 last month, the Buy Amount changes to 15 to indicate you need to buy 15 more now.

Although you already understand what you need to do with the worksheet, here's a basic process you'll go through:

1. Enter in all the information, letting the Amazon link auto-populate from the ASIN field.
2. You'll find the values for In Stock (to the right) in your Inventory section of Amazon Seller Central.
3. Locate sales for the past 30 days in Seller Central. These are in the Orders section. Also, you can look at your Restock Inventory Report. Capture screen shots throughout (or a video) to use for a VA later.

   Tip: With the suggested Buy Amount column calculating for you, you can sort the sheet by that column, high to low, to quickly see all the items that need to be bought and shipped right now.

   Note: The worksheet lets you keep track of your goals as well. If your replen goal for this stage, based on the return numbers you're averaging, is 200 items, you could color highlight the 201st row when you start using the worksheet. When you finally get there and add the replen that fills that colored row, you will have reached that stage's milestone.

4. Outsource the worksheet's management to a VA as soon as possible.

A Turnkey Replen Management System for You

I've mentioned our Replen Management software a few times before and you can find it here:

www.replendashboard.com

Amazon Arbitrage and Wholesale Seller Inventory Headaches Solved

Replen Dashboard accurately tracks product movement and trends to help you with buying decisions and inventory projections.

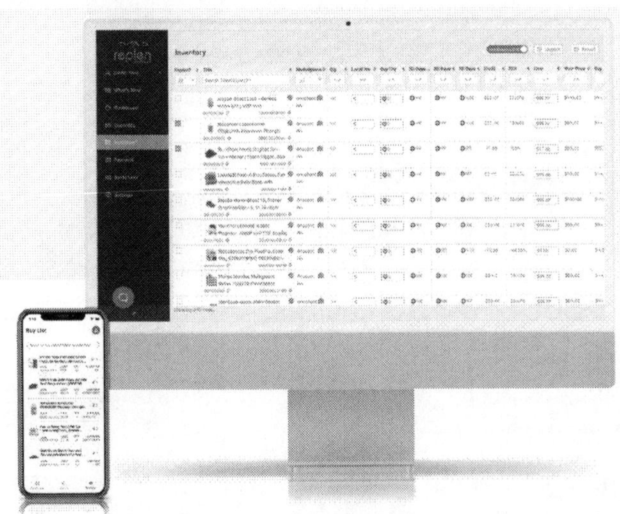

Sign up for a free month's trial so that you won't risk funds trying the software. Karl Jacobi, Greg Flint, and I developed the software from the ground up to manage every aspect of replens inventory *specifically for ourselves and for you.* The replen management system is the most powerful *and simplest* method you'll find to manage replens. If you use it early, it works for you and continues to do so as you grow large.

The Replen Dashboard software connects to your Amazon account and grabs all the Amazon-hosted data automatically. The software is hosted in the cloud and maintains all lists there and not on your computer, so you won't be limited to a specific machine to work from as you run the software.

A lady named Rachel in our $0 to $100k in Replens Facebook group recently posted that before using the Replen Dashboard software, she paid a VA $50 each and every month to manage her replens. Now, the software does all the work for her, cost less, and doesn't need the routine interaction required to deal with a VA. (Not that a lot of interaction is needed with VAs once they get going. But replacing them when they move on requires a bunch of re-orientation time from you.)

> **Warning:** Whatever you do, do *not* take Amazon Seller Central's advice on replen quantities. Amazon's suggestions have absolutely no meaning in a replenishment system we're describing here.

Additionally, we are constantly adding improvements for our users such as an app for your phone that you can instantly create shopping lists to help you manage your shopping team, buy list functionality for easily creating shipments, local inventory tracking for what's at your warehouse/prep center, and so much more! We have tons of videos for how to use the software as well on my AskJimmySmith Youtube channel and a demo of the software on the website replendashboard.com.

Lastly, if you join the course for this book at www.provenamazoncourse.com/replens you get 10% off FOR LIFE on the Replen Dashboard software after you go through the course.

A Repricer Saves Time and Makes Money

A *repricer* is a software program that monitors your live FBA inventory's prices and changes them as competing sellers change their prices. You control the minimum price, maximum price, and the strategy that your repricer uses to get you the most sales. (Many sellers use their repricers to maintain ownership of the Buy Box. If another seller takes away the Buy Box from you, your repricer will attempt to grab back the Buy Box using guidelines you provide.)

> **Note:** If you just don't want to tackle a repricer yet, that can wait until Stage Three. To newcomers, the concept of finding and setting up a repricer might seem daunting at first. While somewhat true that the more effort you put into

> fine-tuning a repricer produces better results and therefore more profit, many repricers are not difficult to get the basics set up. As a matter of fact, most of them have preset configurations you select and forget about except for some minor adjustments once in a while.

Repricers work day and night, constantly updating prices for you. The work a repricer does saves you from constantly checking your live inventory's competition and changing prices yourself. You have far more important things to do, such as find new replens.

A good time to subscribe to a repricing service is when you get to 100 items in your inventory. The main one I recommend for sellers is Aura (bit.ly/replensgoaura) because it has more features and is more reliable than other repricers. I also have seen great success for people that use Profit Protector Pro (bit.ly/ppprepricer) which is a bit more inexpensive but as of the time of this writing it is a newer software. If you'd like to see my most up-to-date list of software recommendations you can head over to askjimmysmith.com/best-resources. Luckily, you have two great options to start with! Somewhere towards the beginning of Stage Two, you'll reach 100 replens. At that time, save time and money by subscribing to a repricer.

> **Note:** If a price starts to tank, your repricer is faster than you to drop your price just enough to sell before moving down more. This means you sell far more than if you don't notice the tanking until you can only sell at a loss. You control the strategy. Perhaps you want the repricer never to drop your price below a certain limit. If the price quickly tanks and the item starts selling for less than your minimum price, your repricer will maintain your lowest price until (hopefully) the low sellers sell out and the price moves back up again.

Let the Grind Commence!

This ends the Stage Two chapter.

You might wonder why Stage One took several chapters to get you from $0 to $10,000 but this stage that takes you four times as far to $40,000 but was described in a single chapter.

First, one obvious reason is the $0 part of Stage One's $0 to $10,000. Getting any new venture started takes training, encouragement, and understanding. Maybe you needed the Keepa training or Keepa review. You had to learn all the concepts related to a replen business.

I opened this chapter telling you that Stage Two is the grinding stage. That's most of it. You've got to open your throttle wide and increase the number of replens you source to approximately 267 different items in order to achieve $40,000 and start the next stage in the process.

Stage Two is the point where you understand your business's mechanics fairly well after completing Stage One's $10,000 goal. Still, your replen business is small enough that you can use Stage Two to begin planning for the massive growth that's about to take you from $40,000 to $100,000 and beyond.

Stage Two is when you must prepare for that growth (but before you get there) by implementing a replens management system, possibly hiring one or more VAs to help with some of the business, and setting up a documentation process of at least your prep and ship routine in order to more easily hand it over to an employee in Stage Three.

In Stage Two, you're working on your business *and* in your business. It's perhaps the hardest stage. Going forth you'll be freed to spend far more energy *on* your business than *in* it. This is the mark of a "real" business who understands entrepreneurial practices. Your ultimate goal is to make yourself completely unneeded in your own business. At that point, you have many options available that you'll never have if you're so critical to the day-to-day workings of your business that you never have any free time to do anything but manage, source, prep, and ship.

It's time to grind out those replens, organize your business, and prepare for the massive growth you're about to experience.

Part 4
–
Stage Three: From $40,000 to $70,000

Chapter 11
–
Stage Three: Moving from $40,000 to $70,000 in Replens

Don't be overwhelmed by Stages Three and Four, especially if you're still on Stage One. Reading ahead is good but doing so might make you fear Stages Three and Four. You'll be fine, you can do this. Each stage is simple, just not always easy. We found Stage Three to be *easier* than the previous two and I believe you will too.

Your replens journey is doable. It's *not* something to worry over.

> "The reason why worry kills more people than work is that more people worry than work."
> ~ Robert Frost

Focus on the stage you're in, even if reading ahead. Hitting $70,000 in sales at the end of Stage Three is *far* less work than seven times the effort you put in to reach Stage One's $10,000.

Again, Brittany and I moved from Stage Two to Stage Three at the $25,000 monthly sales level. We didn't wait until we were at $40,000. You may or may not be able to do this. You may want to do this at $25,000 or even before if you have the capital. I believe $40,000 is the top of the range for anyone in Stage Two. Past $40,000, you *must* move to Stage Three.

Stage Three is where you get smarter. *Much* smarter. And not coincidentally, you should get wealthier too.

To give you some confidence, Stage Three is the stage Brittany and I accomplished the quickest.

Stage Three is where you kick in the entrepreneurial mindset. To reach Stage Three's $70,000 per month goal, you must and will begin thinking like an entrepreneur instead of thinking like a worker, an employee, or even a business owner.

> **Note:** Business owners often work harder than everybody else in their own business. Business owners who are entrepreneurial in their mindset, however, begin to work smarter in their businesses. *That's* how you grow your replens business to $70,000 now, then bump it to $100,000+ in the next stage.

When people first begin, the idea of hiring even one part-time helper seems daunting and impossible. Early on, training others is almost impossible because you don't even know the business yourself. Also, you may have no capital to invest in another person so the little you have goes straight into new inventory.

Stage Three becomes a leveling stage for new resellers who started with a shoestring budget *and* those who had plenty of capital to invest. Your replen sales start to bring your business nice capital to increase inventory and improve the way you do everything. You'll spend less time prepping and shipping replens because you'll find somebody to do the more tedious work like that. You'll be helping them earn income and you'll be working far smarter by freeing up your time to find more replens.

More of your time will be managing and less physically working. With rare exception, you can't grow at this point doing everything by yourself.

> **Note:** We're going to ease your replen math this stage. This makes it easier to get more replens faster.

You don't *have* to modify your numbers, such as dropping your minimum ROI to 25 or 30%, but with your new capital levels, you'll be able to afford the smaller ROI and still hit your $70,000 target on time.

Stage Three's most important job is the hiring of one or more employees. I get asked the most questions in this stage about hiring in my "$0 to $100k in Replens" Facebook group, so I'm going to dedicate the next chapter to the hiring process.

For the rest of this chapter, let's discuss Stage Three's non-hiring aspects.

You'll Need a Dedicated Space and Systems in Place

Stage Three is when you'll get a dedicated prep and ship space. It doesn't *necessarily* mean a warehouse or rented office space, but it needs to be moved out of your living room or spare bedroom if you're still working there. If you worry about rent costs, once again this is the stage, we grew the fastest. We directly attribute it to getting help and moving to a dedicated space.

A dedicated space lets you make needed changes. Install shelving to hold boxes, set up workspaces for prepping and shipping, and add racks to hold inventory without interfering with home activities. You can use a warehouse, office space, garage, barn, storage center, and just about anywhere else you dedicate to your business as long as you *stop using your home.*

> **Note:** Sure, the garage is part of your home but if you fully dedicate it to your business and not share it with parking cars or family things, a garage can get you through major growth. Think ahead about weather; if your garage gets cold or hot or both, you and your employees will have problems. You'll need to install insulation and a heating/cooling system.

You're not moving just for the dedicated space. You're moving out of your home for your mindset too. As you grow, you'll focus more and more on the business. You must be able to get away from it all once in a while. That's healthy and enables you to keep perspective on what's important and when it's important.

The constant thinking of prices and replen purchases and sales and shipments and employees and VAs and replenishing supplies all make it difficult to recharge your mind and body. You won't give attention to daily family relationships. If your business still resides in your home when you hire your first employee, that person will be there a lot. That impacts your family time no matter how well you get along with the employee.

Moving out of your house requires that you trust your employees and grow your business by sourcing while your employees work on prepping and shipping.

> **Tip:** We found a warehouse the size we wanted by searching Craigslist. When we googled warehouse space, we found huge warehouses that had far more space (and cost!) than we wanted. Search Craigslist to find appropriate space. You can drive around industrial parks in areas you'd like to rent in and see what's available there as well.

When You Lease a Space, Put These in Place

If you've never leased a commercial space, you might not know all that's required of you. The following items are a priority when you lease:

- Insurance on building and contents – Floods and fire makes insurance a must. Most commercial office or warehouse locations require you get building and contents insurance as terms in your lease.
- Workers' Comp insurance – You'll need to protect your employees; it's surprisingly inexpensive.
- Equipment and Supplies – You'll need computer equipment, Internet access, shipping supplies, prep tools, cameras for security and employee monitoring, tables, chairs, and so on. The cameras not only monitor whether or not your employees are being accurate with their time, but cameras reduce other discrepancies, such as false accusations and so on.

You now have extra time to work on your lease and these kinds of requirements because in Stage Three you have an employee or two, a VA, and part of the business that used to consume your time is now on autopilot.

Shop a Lot, You're Headed to $70,000 per Month!

You'll be prepping and shipping far less (or never again, *yay!*) but many replen sellers tell me they exchange much of that time to shop for more replens. They do this because they enjoy it and they've refined the skills to expert levels. Stage Three's relaxed return requirements make finding inventory easier than ever before.

Others spend some Stage Three time training a new shopper to find replens for them instead of increasing shopping time they themselves do.

Remember Our Timeline

I realize I keep stressing it, but when we hired employees our sales went from $25,000 to the next month of $39,000 followed by $73,000. That's $25,000 to $73,000 in two months. We went extremely quickly through this stage *only* because we could now focus on shopping, shopping, shopping.

Stage Three's Math

Here are the numbers you want to get to by the end of Stage Three.

Maintain at least a $15 ASP. This means you'll need to sell 4,667 items each month to reach the target $70,000 in sales ($70,000 / $15 = 4,667 units).

> **Note:** See why I warned you in this chapter's opening words not to fear Stage Three if you're still in Stage One? 4,667 sales each month seems like a massive goal only because *it is a massive goal!* But it's a massive goal that's 100% obtainable by Stage Three.

An average of 10 sales each month requires that you move up to a total of 467 different replens. That's 467 SKUs. That's up to 467 items that need to be bought and restocked each and every month. Good thing you have help now, isn't it?

At finding 30 replens per month, Stage Three takes you about 16 months to hit $70,000 in sales if there aren't major replen drop-offs. That 16-month estimate considers an average 5% dropoff rate into account.

If 16 months seems like a long time, it's actually a *reasonable* and *conservative* time frame that's completely doable. When we went from $39,000 to $70,000 in one month, we had no training manual to follow. You're holding your training manual right now.

In one month.

That's a major growth stage and the very same thing can happen with your business. 16 months to hit Stage Three is extremely conservative. Many will even get to Stage Four far faster.

> **Note:** I won't stop stressing this to you: mindset becomes more and more important as you become more and more successful.

Stage Three Tools

Continue using all the tools you used in Stage Two. None drop out with the exception of upgrading some, such as replacing a paper replen management system with the Google worksheet I offered, or better, utilizing the Replen Dashboard software at replendashboard.com.

If you didn't get a repricer in Stage Two, you must get one immediately. Don't wait any longer, subscribe to a repricer service. To see my latest recommendations for a repricer go to askjimmysmith.com/best-resources. Amazon does have a free repricer built into Seller Central, but it has absolutely no robust customization features that someone at the Stage Three level might utilize.

At your inventory levels, you can afford to get an even more robust repricer than my typical recommendations such as Informed.co (which is what we use in our business.) These and other advanced repricer models have employees who will interview you and walk you through the initial setup. (Informed.co will even set up the repricer's parameters for you as they talk with you on the phone.) Therefore, you have no excuse not to use one.

> **Tip:** If you began using a repricer in Stage Two and like the job it's doing, I suggest you spend some time on the repricer's web site watching some of the advanced tutorial videos. Search YouTube for customer videos that show how they use your repricer. You'll get great tips and make your existing repricer more powerful.

Repricers keep your items selling when prices move down a bit and increase your profits when prices move up. In other words, a repricer acts like your own VA, adjusting prices according to simple rules you set up.

> **Note:** Some resellers fear that a repricer will ride prices down if an item begins to tank. Although technically it can happen, what you'll more often find is that your repricer gets you sold *out* of inventory right at the top of a price tanking slide. It's virtually impossible to tell when a price is tanking if you're adjusting your own prices. Your repricer won't miss any sudden price swings and can either get you out of a tanking market early or immediately boost your selling price when a shortage occurs and prices rise rapidly.

If you don't have a repricer yet, your business will flow better if you get one immediately. But if you're reading ahead before you've reached Stage Three, get a repricer when you reach 100 items of inventory *or* if you have the extra funds, subscribe to one earlier. They aren't extremely costly with some prices starting at $25 per month.

> **Note:** Brittany and I didn't begin using a repricer until we had more than 300 SKUs. Honestly, we waited far too long. We show that you *can* grow without one, but I don't suggest you trying it.

After signing up for a repricer, read the introductory help screens, watch the videos, and if the repricer's team offers an introductory phone call as many do, definitely take advantage of that to get your account set up initially.

Here are some general parameters we focus on:

- Match the Buy Box – We set up our repricers to match the Buy Box price as long as prices don't dip below our preset minimum for that item. For non-replens, this isn't always the best option, but for replens your goal is boredom! You want to rely on about the same number of items selling each month. If you priced above the Buy Box, then the Buy Box might not rise to hit your replen's price for several weeks. Unless an item is a seasonal replen, you want sales as consistently as possible. Your plan always is to restock monthly, sell out monthly, and rinse and repeat as long as the item's financial returns stay stable. The Buy Box gets the sale most of the time.
- Reprice 3% below Amazon's price – We don't source replens that have Amazon on the listing a lot. If Keepa shows Amazon jumping on and off but not staying long, we will. Don't let Amazon's random appearance bother you if you can stay within your profit requirements at Amazon's historic prices.

  When Amazon jumps on a listing, Amazon is selfish with that Buy Box. Amazon drops the price if necessary to grab the Buy Box. Amazon does reward many resellers who offer a fair, competitive price by releasing the Buy Box throughout the time they share it with us.

  Amazon is fairly good at sharing the Buy Box with resellers who price 3% or more below Amazon's price. That's why you want to tell your repricer to stay 3% less than Amazon when Amazon jumps on the listing. You should get your share of sales even though Amazon's there with you for a time.
- Reprice 10% above MF – When you're the only FBA seller on an item sold by Merchant Fulfilled sellers, Instruct your repricer to price 10% above the lowest MF price. FBA sellers almost always find it possible to command 10% over MF sellers because Amazon Prime buyers prefer to buy from FBA sellers with free shipping.

- Manually input your own Min and Max prices – When you set up a repricer, you can select a formula to determine the lowest and highest price the repricer can change an item's price to. You could tell the repricer that all minimum prices should remain 15% or higher ROI and that all maximum prices can go as high as 200% ROI for example.

  Instead of the formulaic approach, we enter each and every minimum and maximum price for each item in our inventory. This takes more time to add an item to our repricer, but we prefer the control. Entering each min and max price enables us to use different percentage parameters on different items instead of using the same formula for every item.

  > **Note:** Think about the following: prices once in a while shoot up extremely fast and drop right back down. They can tank down and back just as fast. We don't want any item's minimum price to drop much below what Keepa says it generally falls to. If we're using a formula for repricing, our repricer takes down our price on rare dips and we could sell out there. By setting our own min and max prices, we ride out unusual price dips and we're prepared when the price goes back to its usual range.

  With the manual minimum and maximum pricing, we do a CSV upload into our repricing software so we can do them in bulk. It only takes us a few minutes to set these up and it's worth not having any issues with our repricer being too aggressive if we were to have a formula approach similar to the one mentioned above. A 15% minimum ROI can be too aggressive on many items, while a 200% maximum ROI can be too low on many items. We will regularly source products that cost a few dollars where we can make 400% ROI on it. If we have our repricer set to using this formula, it will automatically lower our maximum price to a 200% ROI and cost us money that we should have made on that product.

Chapter 12
–
Hiring Employees

We hired help at the $25,000 monthly sales level. (If you're reading ahead and haven't hired yet, you will when you get to this stage.) Plan to spend about a week training your first employee(s) and then let them run with the job. If you haven't hired yet, do so now. The time saved and the money earned will make you glad you did even if six months ago you never dreamed you'd have a business with hired employees.

> **Note:** Most people in my $0 to $100k in Replens Course agree that Stage Three is the quickest growth stage when reaching $100,000 in monthly sales.

Many not only find Stage Three to be the quickest stage in their growth, they also say it's the most fun. You've had to do a lot of work to this point (unless you had lots of capital to get help earlier). Your time will be greatly freed up now to use more creatively and effectively.

Where to Find Employees

One of the main concerns is where to find employees. For prep and ship workers, I suggest: friends and family, Facebook postings, the NextDoor app (a local app that can be narrowed down so your posts are seen only around your immediate neighborhood), church bulletin announcements, community organization bulletins (YMCA, etc.), colleges, high schools, Craigslist, and help wanted ads.

> **Note:** I listed the order from easiest to hardest. Friends and family offer an easier pool to choose from if for no other reason than they're known to you unlike somebody who answers a help wanted ad.

Here is exactly what we post when we want to hire somebody:

> Hey Everyone – Our company is expanding! We are looking to get a couple of part time employees to work on prepping and shipping products for us. We pay $XX an hour. It is air conditioned and has flexible hours. Looking for someone who could work long term and possibly be full time down the line. It's a fairly simple job. You must be able to lift 50 pounds and have reliable transportation. We are located in [city], [state]. PM me or comment below if you're interested or if you know someone who is. Thank you!

No matter who you interview, you'll always require a job application. Even if you consider hiring family members, you want a job application. Walk them through a standard application check. You can tell them why; this gives you needed practice for later when you hire outside the family. (A complete stack of job applications and reference checks from *all* hired and rejected applicants can also help document that you were consistent and not discriminatory in some illegal way.)

> **Tip:** We found a job application on Google by searching *job application template.*

Interview each applicant at a Starbucks or Panera Bread to gauge how well you trust the person and also to get a feel for your rapport with them. For the ones that have whatever experience you require (if any) and whom you have a good rapport, take them to your jobsite for a walkthrough tour of what they'll begin doing such as prepping and shipping.

There, we explain our business, tell them how the job they do helps the business, and discuss with them if they think they might like the work. You don't want to find out after you hire somebody that it's work they hate or that they're incapable of doing it for whatever reason. You want to ensure that your location is a location they can consistently get to on time. Discuss whatever other factors come to their minds when they see the job they will do.

If and when the candidate looks like a good fit, explain they will work a 30-day trial period (or whatever time frame works for you). 30 days should be plenty to hire them and get them comfortable enough to work unsupervised before the trial expires.

You'll explain that at the end of their trial period, they'll sit down with you and walk through a review of how they did, discuss both your expectations of them and their expectations of you, and how you might move forward. If everybody is good with that entire process/plan, hire them and let them fill out required documents such as the W-4 form.

A Hiring Checklist

I created a hiring checklist that summarizes all I just discussed about the hiring process.

> Remember, you can download a copy of the checklist and the rest of the resources for this book here: askjimmysmith.com/bookresources

Click to create your own Copy of the checklist which you then can print, download, or save as your own.

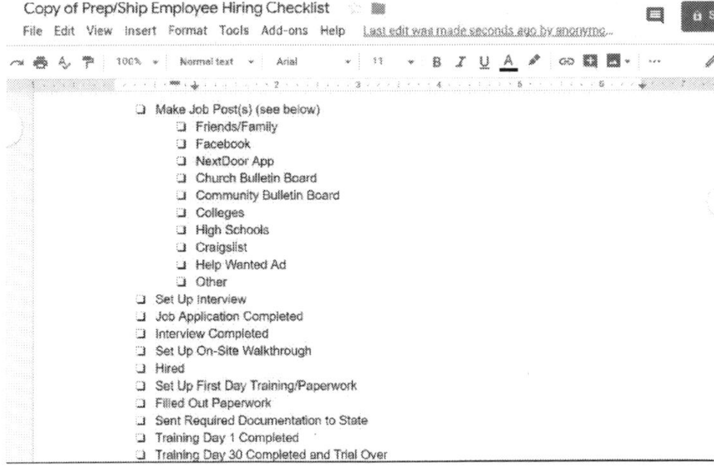

Copy of Prep/Ship Employee Hiring Checklist

File Edit View Insert Format Tools Add-ons Help Last edit was made seconds ago by anonymo...

- ❏ Make Job Post(s) (see below)
  - ❏ Friends/Family
  - ❏ Facebook
  - ❏ NextDoor App
  - ❏ Church Bulletin Board
  - ❏ Community Bulletin Board
  - ❏ Colleges
  - ❏ High Schools
  - ❏ Craigslist
  - ❏ Help Wanted Ad
  - ❏ Other
- ❏ Set Up Interview
- ❏ Job Application Completed
- ❏ Interview Completed
- ❏ Set Up On-Site Walkthrough
- ❏ Hired
- ❏ Set Up First Day Training/Paperwork
- ❏ Filled Out Paperwork
- ❏ Sent Required Documentation to State
- ❏ Training Day 1 Completed
- ❏ Training Day 30 Completed and Trial Over

> **Note:** The posting you read earlier that we put on bulletin boards or online to seek employees appears at the bottom of checklist. Copy and edit the wording to match your requirements.

Employees vs. Independent Contractors

We're extremely cautious. We might go an extra step to safeguard a process. You may or may not want to go to the extremes we do depending on your previous business experience of hiring others.

You have more direct control and responsibility over employees than you have with independent contractors. In fact, you don't actually hire independent contractors. You hire the company they work for (or hire from their own company if they're a sole proprietor).

To determine if you want to hire employees or independent contractors, you first and foremost need to know the law. You don't want someone to come in later and inform you that you must switch all your independent contractors to employees. Before setting up your hiring, you've got to know the difference.

What's Required for Employees

When hiring employees as opposed to independent contractors, the following is required:

- They use your training.
- They use your tools and supplies.
- They work according to your direction as to when, where, and how they work.
- They are covered by your company insurance and benefits if you have benefits. Whether or not you have benefits, they're covered by your worker's comp insurance.

What's Required for Independent Contractors

- They know how to do the job already and aren't *primarily* trained by you.

- They can work for others doing the same job as they do for you. We ask our employees to sign a document stating they won't do the same kind of work for others. This is why we hire employees and not independent contractors.
- They get reimbursed for materials and supplies they use and provide themselves. Technically, they're supposed to provide polybags and even FNSKU stickers and you reimburse them.
- They set their own schedule within guideline parameters you set up.
- They aren't covered by company insurance or benefits.

You can do a Google search to get more specific information on the differences or ask an accountant. If you were to pay an accountant a consulting fee to go over all these options and work out the best plan for you, it would probably be worth the cost. This helps ensure you do everything correctly from the beginning.

For us, going the employee route was the clear winner. It would be foolish for a contractor to buy and bring polybags and stickers when we're well stocked. We wanted to control the schedules worked and train them.

Shoppers might be better candidates for independent contractors than prep and ship workers. You don't really care what time of day a shopper buys items. However, we set them up as employees since we train them and have them sign a non-compete.

Documents

Workers require documentation of various kinds.

Employees require the following forms. Google them to locate all of them quickly. You'll be able to download them in .pdf format.

- Federal Form I-9
- Federal Form W-4
- State Forms (for example, my state of Missouri requires a Missouri W-4)
- Google the forms below for your state (each state is different)
  - Employment Contract

- Non-Compete Agreement (optional, but we require it)
- Employee Handbook (each state has different laws on break requirements, lunch requirements, insurance requirements, and so forth)

Independent Contractors require the following forms:

- Federal Form W-9
- Independent Contractor Agreement stating exactly what you expect them to do
- Other state forms might be required (nothing more was required for Missouri-based Independent Contractors)

Scheduling and Payments

The scheduling of employees is up to you. The scheduling of independent contractors is up to them with some guidelines that you two agree to. Independent Contactors can have deadlines, but how they meet those deadlines is generally left to their discretion.

When we started our warehouse we wanted our prep and ship employees to work from 2 to 6pm, Monday through Friday. Now, we have people there between 8 AM & 6 PM but most are still part-time employees that work different shifts. We occasionally ask for more hours worked, such as when we have a huge influx of products that need to get out the door.

We could've hired two full-time employees to do the same work as the four part time ones we originally started with. We felt the part-timers working half days are a little fresher and so it's our personal preference.

For paying employees, I can't give you better advice than to tell you to talk to a trusted accountant (I have my accountant as a recommendation at askjimmysmith.com/best-resources). You don't want to skip something critical for your state.

For the basics, though, here are some general factors to know about paying employees:

- You need to take out Social Security, Medicare, Federal Tax, and State Tax

- An accountant or payroll service will do this for you.
- You're required to match Social Security and Medicare payments for employees.
- You must disclose on each check the following: Gross Pay, everything that's deducted, and the Net Pay. Some of today's employees prefer to be paid with a service such as PayPal and you need to ensure the Notes section includes the required breakdown of the paycheck. (Accountants, bookkeepers, and payroll services will do this for you.)
- We pay every two weeks to reduce time spent making payments. You can pay weekly if you prefer.

Independent contractors require fewer details. For each one who works for you:

- Nothing is taken out of their checks. It's up to the business they work for to handle all the deductions.
- We require invoices *from them* every pay period showing how many hours they worked and the general parameters of what they did. This gives you documentation in case you're audited.

Tracking Hours and Monitoring Employees

We use Google Docs to track employee hours. This includes the Date, Name, Time Started, Time Left, and Total Time for Unpaid Breaks. The Unpaid Break field is for an employee who might be working extra hours one day and takes a break or two for lunch for instance. We ask that they put this break in the Google Doc.

Here is the Google Doc we use. Feel free to copy it and use it for your own purposes, to get the link go here: askjimmysmith.com/bookresources

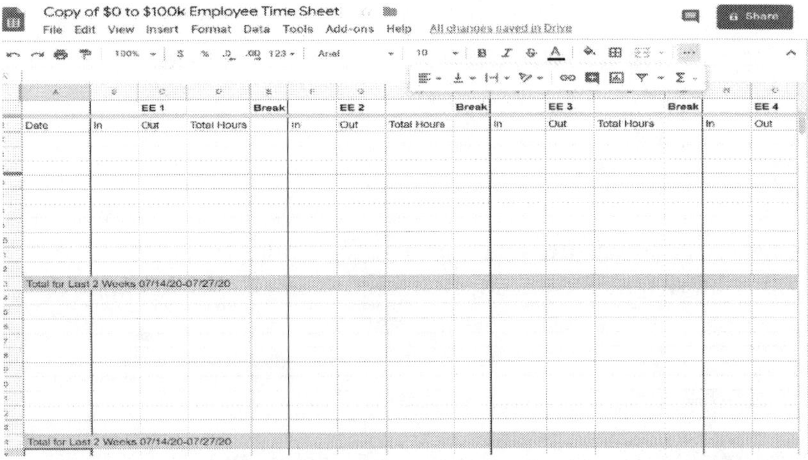

Copy of $0 to $100k Employee Time Sheet

		EE 1		Break		EE 2		Break		EE 3		Break		EE 4
Date	In	Out	Total Hours		In	Out	Total Hours		In	Out	Total Hours		In	Out
Total for Last 2 Weeks 07/14/20-07/27/20														
Total for Last 2 Weeks 07/14/20-07/27/20														

If you use a payroll service, they'll often have employee tracking software and apps you can use.

Finally, we installed cameras in our warehouse to confirm and monitor employee activity. We trust our employees, but especially for new ones, we like to keep track. We have cameras set up in the outside front, outside back, inside front, and inside back. We have cameras on our in-house inventory. We prefer *Blink* cameras for the outside and *Nest* cameras for the inside (our favorite versions of these cameras are in our supplies document at askjimmysmith.com/bookresources).

> **Note:** Blink cameras send us alerts when somebody shows up and we can check on them if we want to. However, we subscribe to a constant, recorded feed with our indoor Nest cameras, so we have a complete record of all warehouse activity.

Resources to Use as You Grow

As our business got bigger, we started to outgrow Google Sheets. You'll hit a point where you'll want to move to paid tools that better help you manage the time tracking, payroll, employee cards, and so on. The time you save by using these services far outweigh the money saved by continuing to use Google Sheets. We have compiled our favorite resources in our resource document at askjimmysmith.com/bookresources. For now, here is an overview of some of what we use in our current business:

- **OntheClock** – We use OntheClock to monitor all our employee's time. It has some amazing features including GPS location for shoppers to check in when they arrive at a store and when they leave. It also has downloads for Gusto (our payroll service below). https://bit.ly/replensOTC
- **Gusto** – Gusto is our payroll service. It's amazing! Gusto saves us hours of time doing our payroll each week and it works well with OntheClock. We both get a $100 Amazon Gift Card when you sign up and use the service! https://bit.ly/replensgusto

The Training Schedule

When we first start, we're with the employee for two weeks and then we're gone for the next two weeks to see how they do. After two weeks of us being there doing the job for them, with them, and then watching them, they're completely up to speed. We let them alone for the final two weeks of their probationary 30 days. This takes us into the one-month review to determine if we're moving forward with them.

> **Tip:** Once you have a running system with multiple trained employees, your longer-term employees can take over the training for you.

Here's the precise training schedule we take with our employees:

- Week one: We're there 100% of the time, walking through shipments and processes.
- Week two: There, but not helping unless something arose they needed guidance with. I suggest you do something in your business that makes sense for you to do while there that second week, such as OA to find new replens. Even if you don't routinely use OA, this is a great use of your time the second week of employee training. You might find you're better at OA than you thought you'd be and start to integrate OA into your replen-finding routine. By being present, questions and unique

problems can be solved, but by not standing next to them the second week, they learn to be more independent.

- Week three: You should be sourcing but stop in to confirm each shipment before it's finalized and shipped to Seller Central.
- Week four: Source outside the warehouse and don't stop by unless required that you do so. They gain full independence at this point *or* they realize the job isn't for them. If the latter happens, you'd rather know now than later.

We get our employees independent of us and they get some errors out of the way with this training schedule. We learn to trust them and they learn to trust us.

Anything to use your time shopping is your ultimate goal at this point.

We expect our employees to be at least 80% as good as we are when they start working by themselves. This means you know they won't be perfect and will make errors, but the errors are few. The mindset that 10-20% might be done in error at first isn't a deal-breaker and by stopping by the third week, you'll spot most problems such as they're not completely sealing polybags or Seller Central shipping labels are on the wrong side of boxes.

As you spot errors, you'll help them improve. Eventually, they will become better at their job than you would be at that same job. This is what you want. This allows you to focus on the things only you can focus on in your business and them to focus on becoming specialists at their jobs.

A Few Words About Our Warehouse Prep and Ship Flow

Each layout will differ depending on your mix of RA and OA and how many items in your replen inventory and how many employees you have. I'll go through our original layout and our current one since we have made it more efficient over time, however for some of you, the old layout/process may make more sense than the new one so that's why I'm including both.

Here's an overview of our old warehouse layout. Use it as a reference while I describe our setup and routines:

Door
Shipment 1 Dropoff
Three Prep Tables
Shipment 2 Dropoff
Shipment 3 Dropoff
Completed/Boxing Area
Bubble Wrap Table
OA Drop Off
Computer/Dymo Table
Supplies/Prep Table
Bubble Wrap/Packing Materials
Weigh Station
Door to Garage

We keep two to three shipments open in InventoryLab that can be added to so that we have three product drop-off areas where shoppers leave items to be prepped. We do this to keep enough product coming in the door to stay two to three shipments ahead of the current shipment. This keeps them busy without overwhelming them in one giant shipment.

> **Tip:** We keep a fourth product drop off area for OA items because we can't as easily control when those arrive. If we add new OA items to one of the existing two or three shipments in progress, it might mess up the flow of that shipment with unexpected additions. By keeping the less reliable OA-timed shipments separate, preppers and packers can grab items from the OA area when they're ready to add to any of the three shipments.

Our old process works like this: our shoppers bring products into the warehouse and leave them at one of the three shipment drop off areas. The warehouse manager (he or she might be your only warehouse employee in the beginning) tells the shoppers which drop off area to leave the products in.

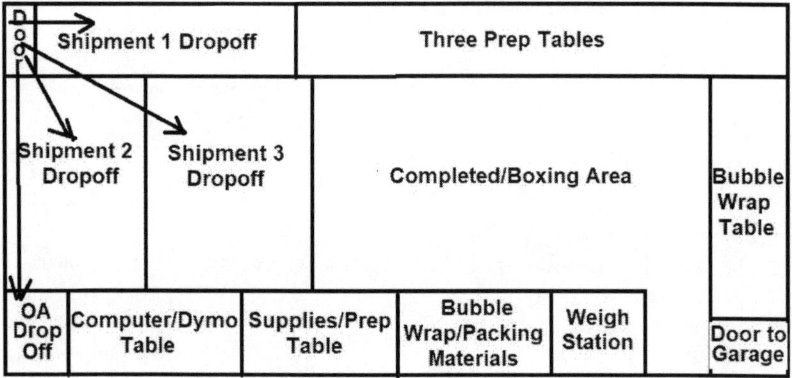

Once the items are dropped off, the Buy List is uploaded for that shipment to InventoryLab. One employee then prints the stickers while another employee splits the items into the appropriate prep stations depending on need (such as bubble wrap required).

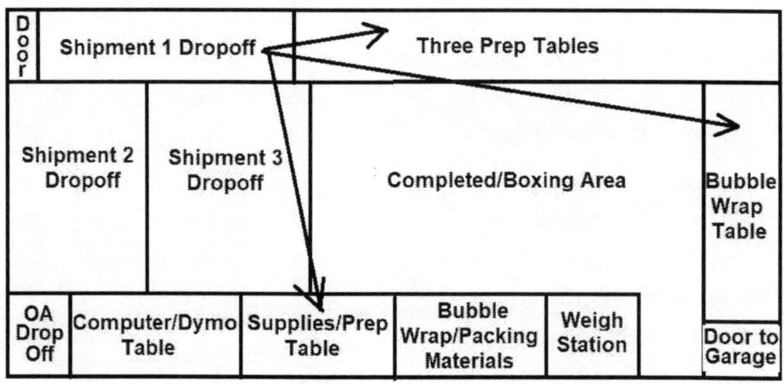

After all the items are prepped, our employees place them in the center of the room where everything there is completely prepped. The entire shipment is completed, submitted to InventoryLab, and Amazon Seller Central accepts the shipment plans before boxes go out the door.

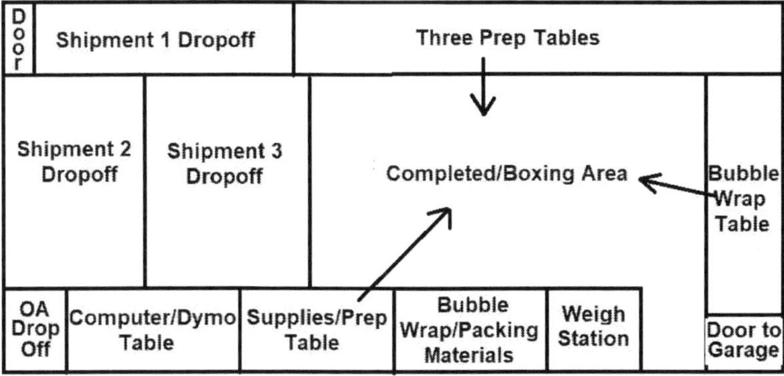

Once the shipment is complete and Seller Central accepts it, the boxes leave for the garage to be picked up by the carrier. Another employee goes back to the drop off area and starts the next shipment.

> **Note:** Our shipments each average about 600 items and we send two to three shipments weekly. We could go higher, but too many products get unwieldy depending on how many employees you have and the way your space is arranged. We used to limit shipments to 300 items to send them in faster, but as our replen inventory grew, 300 wasn't enough.

Now for the new layout/process:

We still keep two to three shipments open in InventoryLab that can be added to so that we have three product drop-off areas where shoppers leave items to be prepped. We do this to keep enough product coming in the door to stay two to three shipments ahead of the current shipment. This keeps them busy without overwhelming them in one giant shipment.

One of those shipments is only for OA so that way as we receive items and place them on the appropriate OA rack(s), we are able to check them in based on that OA shipment.

You'll notice in the below layouts that we have rolling racks now. These racks allow us a few perks. One, they allow us to use vertical space in our warehouse vs having everything spread out along tables or the floor. This greatly increases how many products we can purchase and bring into the warehouse. Two, they are mobile since they roll. This makes it much easier to have one prepping person handle their own rack instead of having to separate out all of the items manually when starting a new shipment. We got these 6 foot tall rolling racks from Sam's Club, but they also have similar ones at Costco. The investment is well worth the time savings plus the ability to have more space in the warehouse. See below for an example of one of them.

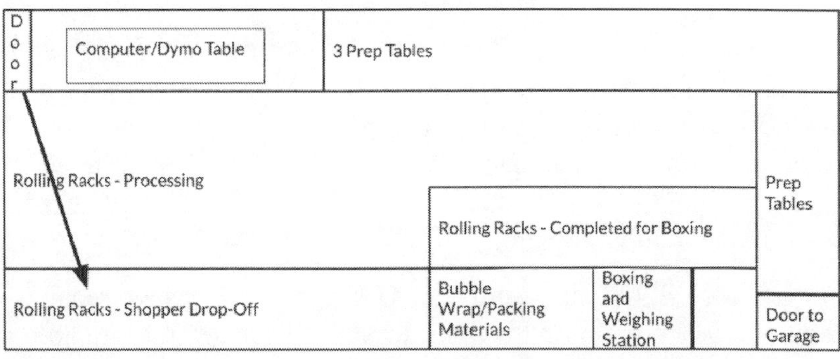

Our new process works like this: our shoppers bring products into the warehouse and leave them on the appropriate rolling rack for that shipment. We separate the racks by shopping day based on color. The color is designated by regular construction paper placed on the rolling rack so the shoppers and prep/ship team can differentiate them. So if it's a Monday, they put it on the blue rack(s), if it's Tuesday, the green rack(s), Wednesday the red rack(s), and so on.

This allows everyone to know which shipment is which because we can name them based on the color coding of the racks. Once the items are dropped off, the Buy List is uploaded for that shipment to InventoryLab.

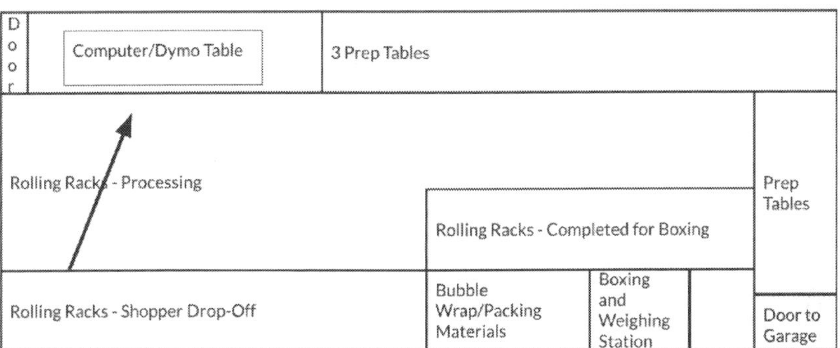

When it's time to do that shipment (since again, we are usually 2 to 3 days ahead of the prep team), one employee then prints the stickers while another employee places the stickers with the appropriate items on the racks. This allows whoever gets that rack for prepping to have the stickers right there with the products and reduces our errors.

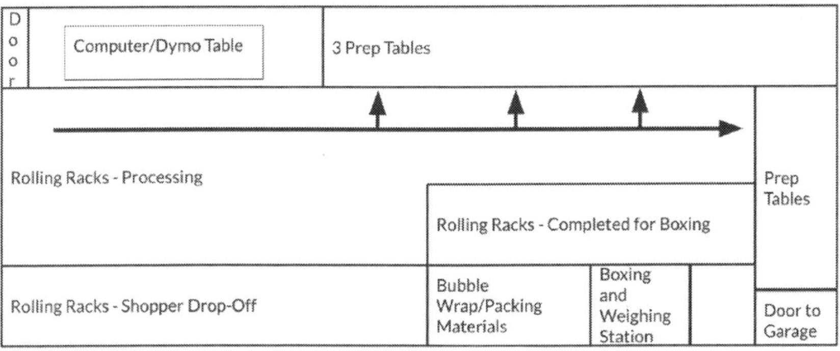

As preppers finish prepping their items, they place the completed items onto "completed" rolling racks that are next to them so they don't have to walk across the room which helps us to speed up this process. When it's time to do the box contents in InventoryLab, the boxing employee knows what is fully finished and what others are working on because the completed items are separated from the ones still needing prep work to be done.

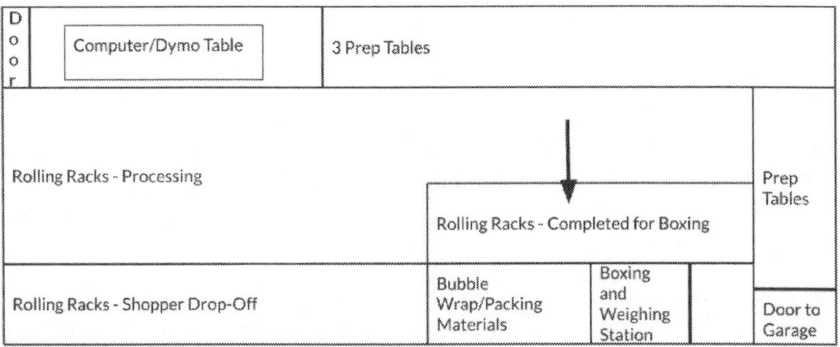

Once the prepping is almost all completed, we have the batch for the shipment in InventoryLab closed out which allows us to start the box content process. The boxing person is able to start boxing everything up while the others are finishing up the prep work.

As the preppers finish their items, they can then start on the next shipment by restarting the process of printing stickers and getting it prepped while the boxing person completes the prior shipment.

The entire shipment is completed from there, submitted to InventoryLab, and Amazon Seller Central accepts the shipment plans before boxes go out the door.

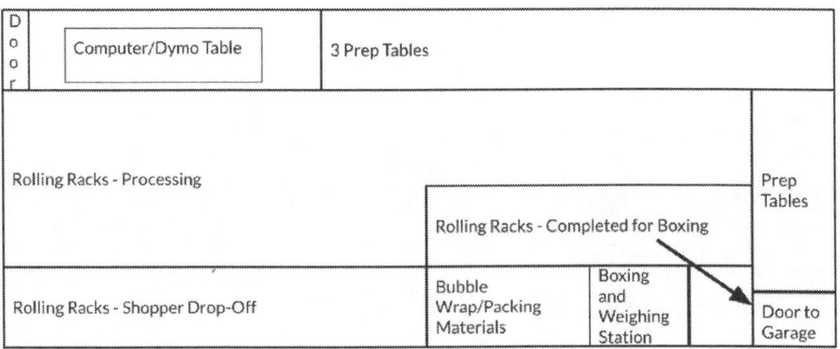

Both the old layout and the new one completely operate without us having to be there. It's up to you to decide what will work best for your business. If you plan on continuing to grow this business, I highly recommend getting some of those rolling racks I mentioned above to help with any space limitations you may have.

Some Extra Prep and Ship Tips

A few related tips come to mind that didn't fit above.

One of my favorite tips for you is to have a card that tells employees when it's time to reorder supplies (typically called a Kanban card.) What we do is put an **X** on a bag or box or bubble wrap for when 25% remains. When they use the polybag right above the **X** card, they reorder that size so that we don't run out.

This means when we first supply a polybag or box size, we literally feel down into the stacks until we're about 25% away from the bottom and put a card with a big **X** on that.

> **Warning:** Running out of supplies is costly. Until you replace them, you can't get shipments out the door to be sold. If this happens, what you'll probably have to do while waiting for the bulk supply order to arrive is send an employee to an office supply store to buy a small quantity at much higher prices than you normally pay for the items. Keeping shipments flowing to Amazon is far more valuable than paying more for temporary supplies.

We have small, rolling carts with a full selection of polybags and other prep supplies each employee keeps stocked and rolls to whatever prep table they're working on. If we didn't use this rolling cart system, we'd need to keep a batch of all prep supplies at the three prep tables. It's far easier to roll the carts over to the supply storage areas for restocking them than to maintain three separate batches of prep supplies at each prepping station.

We used to cover each and every barcode in a multipack or bundle and it consumed a lot of time and stickers. Amazon resellers are used to placing *Sold as Set* stickers on the outside of boxes that weren't to be opened by the FBA warehouse. We now also use

Sold as Set stickers on all bundles and multipacks so we don't have to cover individual barcodes inside those polybags.

For individual items we polybag, we don't cover item barcodes. We place the outside FNSKU sticker over the item's barcode area. Slippage can occur if the item moves around and the inside barcode might display through the bag, but we've never had problems.

Once in a while, OA items arrive damaged and need to be returned and refunded. We have a set-aside location for damaged OA items to be processed.

Instead of our employees sending us multiple calls and texts each day for non-emergency issues that arise, we require that they send a daily recap email to us for any and all non-emergency issues. At the end of the day, we work with the employees to reconcile the issues in the email(s).

> **Note:** The daily recap of non-emergency emails enables us to create or modify written procedures to handle common problems that arise more than once. This way future employees will be able to deal with common problems others had before them.

Part 5
–
Stage Four: From $70,000 to $100,000… and Beyond!

Chapter 13
–
Stage Four: Moving from $70,000 to $100,000 in Replens

If Stage Three was our fastest-moving stage, Stage Four is the most fun stage. The grind is well behind you.

> "Tough times never last, but tough people do."
> ~ Robert H. Schuller

Going forward, you'll find that replenishing items get far more enjoyable.

The way it got to be fun is that we outsourced our work even more. Instead of just getting help with prepping and shipping, we got shoppers to purchase existing replens. We started to think bigger because we now had time, capital, experience, and confidence to know what we were doing and that we could continue growing our replens. We used some of our relief from business-required time and efforts to plan a broader picture of where we wanted to go.

We finally had the mindset, time, and capital to explore new avenues such as wholesale. (Yes, you can buy replens wholesale and we'll talk about this before the book ends.) At Stage Four, you begin to make considerations you never would have before. *Should we work more to find the needed replens or do we want to hire one or more people and train them to buy new replens? Should we consider adding more OA sourcing for our replens? Do we want to hire VAs (Virtual Assistants) to source OA or do we want to hire one or more people from our local area as employees to source OA?*

You Might Have Too *Much* Capital!

Who would have thought too much capital would be a problem?

You have all the money coming in that you've been working so hard for. The problem is that finding new replens to spend all the money on is harder because there's extra money! We spent some to hire a person to manage our replen inventory. By this time, we had a VA handle tasks such as reimbursements and negative feedback.

> **Note:** If you head over to askjimmysmith.com/best-resources you can see my recommended VA service for helping you get money back from Amazon that they owe you.

By the way, one of our employee's jobs is to look at all past replens that dropped off to see if the price or number of sellers now makes those replens worth adding back. Such recycling of drop-offs produces plenty of renewed replens to make that time worth the effort. Renewing an older replen ends up being easier than finding a new one much of the time because you know it's history, where to source it, and how many should sell better than you did when you first tested it.

We even hired a personal shopper to get our family groceries to reduce time we spent doing that. That's the difference between owning a job by being a business owner and being an entrepreneur. Entrepreneurs strive to make his or her *time* more valuable. An entrepreneur constantly seeks ways to reduce time spent on any task that someone else can do just as well. I highly recommend using any of the multitude of services/apps out there to offload some of these tedious tasks. Apps like Doordash, Instacart, Shipt, TaskRabbit, etc. will help you to save so much time to spend on other things for a nominal fee when compared to how much money you should be making in this replens business.

In addition to capital management, you'll also be honing your systems in Stage Four. Part of your capital is perhaps renting a larger location for your growing inventory and prep center.

> **Note:** Our employee costs run about 10% of total sales. You can use this as a general rule for your business.

The $100,000 Math

At an ASP of $15, you will sell about 6,667 units each month ($100k / $15 = 6,667 monthly sales). At 10 sales per month on the average, that means you'll be required to sell about 667 different replens.

It takes 23 months at the continued rate of 30 replens in 30 days. This doesn't account for drop-offs and I'll remind you we have about 5% of our replens drop off and need replacing each month.

> **Note:** At this level of sales, the 5% drop-off rate becomes significant. A 5% drop-off rate equates to about 30 replens monthly that you'll lose. Therefore, you'll source twice as many new replens monthly than before to maintain your growth, all things being equal.

I like to give you a conservative growth rate first. Here, the math requires that it will take 23 months to reach the golden $100,000 per month target.

The math assumes everything remains constant, but nothing really remains constant. You might have more or fewer drop-offs. Your sourcing skills may have increased enough to find far more replens each month with far less effort. You might hire more shoppers to find replens for you, thus greatly increasing the rate at which your business adds new replens.

As our timeline showed, we went from $30,000 to $100,000 in nine months (not counting the highly skewed fourth quarter where sales naturally topped $100,000 due to the seasonal boost). The complete growth of our replens business took a year and a half to move from $0 to $100,000.

And I didn't have this book as a guide! I hope you succeed far faster, as many of my students have.

Hiring Shoppers

Hiring shoppers is definitely the most critical part of Stage Four and it's important you understand that process. Therefore, hiring shoppers consumes much of this chapter.

With Stage Four's replen levels, this is when you hire one or more shoppers. Much of what you need to know about hiring shoppers is similar to what you learned about hiring prep and ship staff (chapter 12). That is, you'll find shoppers in the same places you looked for preppers and shippers: friends and family, Facebook posts, the NextDoor app, church bulletins, community organization bulletins, colleges, high schools, Craigslist, and help wanted ads.

Additionally, you can look for people that already work with Instacart, Shipt, and other shopping services/apps. They already know many of the stores and they're typically easy to spot since many wear the shirts of the company they're with while they're shopping. They can make much more money with you than they do with these apps as well, especially if you train them how to source.

Once you find someone interested in the job, have them fill out a job application that you find online and interview them to see how well you gauge mutual trust. Shoppers will have access to a credit card and possibly discounted gift cards that you let them use. They are higher risk for you than preppers and shippers. (We'll discuss how they buy products a little later in this chapter.)

In the interview, you'll need to discuss what they'll do using examples. It's good to extend part of the interview to an actual store. Walk them through the kinds of things they will do for you.

Will you regularly supply them with a shopping list for restocking inventory? That's fairly straightforward. They get a list of things to buy and where to buy them and a price range to stick with and they go get the items. If you use Replen Dashboard as mentioned earlier, it comes with an app to make this even easier for you. If not, you can use the Google Sheet example I provided for your shoppers as well.

Will you also train them to find new replens? (You should once you fully trust them.) If so, that's huge and you need to be specific because people new to this business might have a totally different idea of what finding products to sell means. Even before you hire them, go through an example or two of how to find replens. Go to the haircare aisle and source a Suave shampoo and conditioner bundle for example. This gives them a far better idea of what the job entails versus what they might think if you only describe the task.

> **Note:** Once, we were all ready to hire a shopper and she wanted to work for us. We did a store walkthrough before committing and she told us that shopping wasn't something she would like to do. We didn't hire her. We'd rather know this *before* we hired her than after! If we'd hired her, filled out all the paperwork, and spent time to train her only for her to quit in a week, that would be a lot of time and effort and money down the drain.

All the tax and legal documents you must fill out for preppers and shippers apply to shoppers. Whereas a non-compete agreement isn't as critical for prep and ship help, it's more so for shoppers. You don't want shoppers buying inventory for their own business or for other Amazon sellers they work for based on anything they learn working for you. Your inventory of replens is your most valuable business asset because that's what generates $100,000 in monthly sales. It doesn't take too many competitors to jump on your replens to start dropping them out of a profitability range.

> **Warning:** When you search Google for a non-compete agreement, be sure to search for one in your state. Each state's non-competes differ. A generic one won't do, get one specifically designed for your state.

Our non-compete agreements run for two years. Workers can't compete for up to two years of leaving our employment. Some businesses don't do this, but we felt more comfortable having them fill out this paperwork before we trained them on our business.

Finally, you'll want to run a 30-day Shopper trial period as you did with the prep and ship crew.

I have a checklist for you to run when hiring a shopper similar to the one I gave you for the prep and ship staff. You can download the checklist and all of the other resources for the book here: askjimmysmith.com/bookresources

The shopper hiring checklist is identical to that of the prep and ship hiring checklist except for the ad you post for the job. Here is how your shopping ad should read:

> Hey Everyone! We really need another shopper for our business and what better way to find one than through an acquaintance or friend here on Facebook?! The deal is simple: extremely flexible hours, day or night, you'd have the ability to bring your kid along with you if need be, you'd be shopping from a predetermined list, must be willing to travel around [City], [State] [or area towns listed as City1, City2, City3, City4, and City5, etc.], travel to our warehouse in [Warehouse Area/Location] for weekly drop offs, must be okay purchasing large quantities of items, and have an SUV/van style of vehicle. Your pay will be $X/hour for training and increases to $X/hour after that. Please message me or comment here if you or a friend might be interested in an interview. Thank you!

Once you hire a shopper, his or her training schedule looks a lot like that of your prep and ship new hires. You'll stay with the new shopper for two weeks and then leave them alone, while still available, for the final two weeks of training.

The first week we're with them in the aisles, finding replens, adding purchased items to the Buy List, using the Replen Dashboard app, and everything else. They need to be studying Keepa (this book's Keepa chapter should suffice along with your own in-store training) if they'll be searching for new replens.

For their second week, we shop with them but in a different part of the store. If they're buying from a list, we're in another part of the store buying restocked items and searching for replens.

On their third week, they shop on their own, but you'll be available for text and phone questions. In some cases, you may need to drive to where they're shopping if they need extra help. They can begin to get anxious when completely on their own shopping and may need assurance. Buying items with someone else's payment method is quite a responsibility. If and when a shopper takes that duty extra seriously, even possibly being hesitant to be on their own until you reassure them some, it's usually a sign that they care.

The idea is for them to be extremely independent by the fourth week knowing they can contact you for advice if needed. Obviously, they can contact you any time after that if there's a problem, but if they get through week four fairly well, they're on their way to independence by the end of that week.

Communication

Obviously when you only have 1 or 2 employees you can communicate through text fairly easily. However, as you grow, you will want to incorporate some sort of company-wide messaging system. Email can be too cumbersome and slow from a response time standpoint, but luckily there are a bunch of different phone app options that also have computer apps tied to them so they will work for whatever the employee uses the most for their job.

We currently use WhatsApp in our business. However, you could use Slack or any other similar messaging service. The apps are free up to a certain point and give an excellent, centralized option for keeping everyone in the loop. Both options currently have desktop versions available as well for anyone that may need it. We have 2 main channels in our business: one for shoppers and one for prep/ship. This allows us to communicate the proper messages and information to the people that need it most – the shoppers don't need to know what the prep/ship people need to know and vice versa in most scenarios, so it's best to separate them and also reduce the clutter that you would have if you had everyone on the same channels.

Our warehouse will use WhatsApp for things such as asking how to prep a new item that may be different than they're used to, if their having issues with software programs, if there are issues with FBM orders, etc. Our shoppers will use WhatsApp if there are pricing changes happening to specific products, if they are having difficulty finding a specific item in the store, to alert us if they are having any issues checking out, etc. If something is extremely urgent, then they are free to call us at any time if necessary.

We do recommend having a daily recap email from your warehouse however. This helps us to keep track of items prepped, shipments completed, shipments working on, and any other odds and ends that can wait until the end of the day email. The WhatsApp messaging channels are more for urgent matters, where the email is for a once-per-day recap of important information, but not urgent.

Scheduling and Payments

Shoppers have more flexibility when they work so we generally let them shop when it's good for them. If you'd prefer they work specific hours, you're entitled to require that. We feel shoppers like the flexibility to work around children's school hours for example.

We pay shoppers every two weeks starting at $11 per hour (at the time of this writing) during training and moving them up to $12 per hour after the first 30 days of training. This gives them an incentive to learn the job during the 30 days, so they keep it at the higher rate.

If they continue to prove themselves, we give them another raise a few months after that. Once you trust them well enough to take over part of your shopping business, they are people you want to keep.

The cost of shoppers averages about 8% of what they purchase (the buy cost). If they spend $1,000, we're paying about $80 for their time in the store. Here's the formula we use for their salary:

Hours Worked x Pay Rate = Pay

Their Pay / Dollars they Spend = Percent of Buy Cost

We always hold to 10% or less on the average, but we rarely see the cost go higher than 8%. This gives you some room to offer bonuses to better shoppers. If they shop fast and accurately and therefore their costs stay at the 8% or less levels, you can incentivize them by offering them a commission of up to 10% to let them control some of what they earn.

If you'd rather not go the commission route, you certainly can bump them up a dollar an hour every few months and that works as an incentive as well.

I'll provide you a Shopper Timesheet example and the other documents for this book here: askjimmysmith.com/bookresources

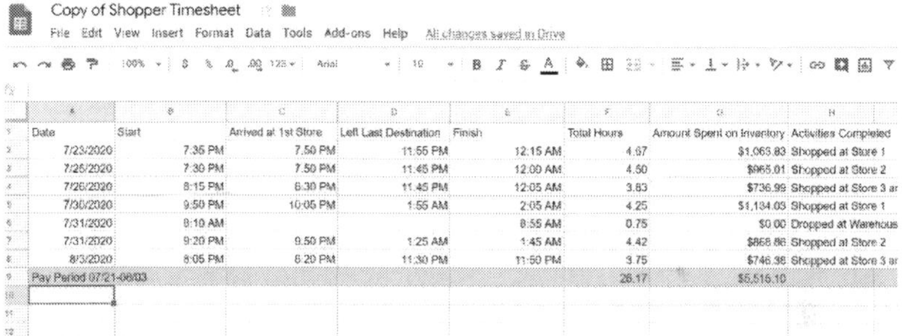

Copy of Shopper Timesheet

File Edit View Insert Format Data Tools Add-ons Help All changes saved in Drive

Date	Start	Arrived at 1st Store	Left Last Destination	Finish	Total Hours	Amount Spent on Inventory	Activities Completed
7/23/2020	7:35 PM	7:50 PM	11:55 PM	12:15 AM	4.67	$1,063.83	Shopped at Store 1
7/26/2020	7:30 PM	7:50 PM	11:45 PM	12:00 AM	4.50	$965.01	Shopped at Store 2
7/26/2020	8:15 PM	8:30 PM	11:45 PM	12:05 AM	3.83	$736.99	Shopped at Store 3 ar
7/30/2020	9:50 PM	10:05 PM	1:55 AM	2:05 AM	4.25	$1,134.03	Shopped at Store 1
7/31/2020	8:10 AM			8:55 AM	0.75	$0.00	Dropped at Warehous
7/31/2020	9:20 PM	9:50 PM	1:25 AM	1:45 AM	4.42	$868.86	Shopped at Store 2
8/3/2020	8:05 PM	8:20 PM	11:30 PM	11:50 PM	3.75	$746.38	Shopped at Store 3 ar
Pay Period 07/21-08/03					28.17	$5,516.10	

We pay them for their drive time from home, so the Start time is the time they leave their house. This is fair in case they live far from the store you send them to. They'll record the time they arrive at the store. This way, you monitor how long it's taking them to get to the store in case that becomes an unusual cost for you. The "Left Last Destination" column is when they leave the store and the Finish time is when they return home.

They'll record the total hours and the dollar amount they spent on inventory that trip. Notice also we pay them for the drop off time to deliver their shopping bags to the warehouse.

As you grow, you will want to switch to a service that I mentioned earlier called OnTheClock. This is what we use to manage our employee time sheets now. For shoppers, it is particularly useful since we can have them check in when they get to a store and it captures their GPS location so we KNOW that they are at least at the store. It is also the most affordable time clock service I've seen that has some great features. You can get it at bit.ly/replensOTC

Monitoring Shoppers

Trust is always a factor with shoppers. You'll want to trust but also verify from time to time. This is why we like to start with friends and family. Although anyone can take advantage of you and family is no exception, you have a known track record with them and it's less risk to put your trust in someone you know as opposed to someone you've never met and know nothing about.

One of the best ways to monitor our shoppers is based on our own experience. By the time you get to the start of Stage Three you know how long it takes to perform restock shopping and finding new replens. Rarely does anyone work as hard in your business than you did the first two stages.

By the time you hire shoppers, you'll be extremely entrenched and have a good feel for what it's like to be a shopper. You'll have almost a sixth sense of what it'll take an average shopper to buy on a certain list of items because you've done it yourself before.

> **Note:** We don't expect a shopper to do as well as we can, but we certainly expect them to become 85% to 90% as efficient as we are.

The data is all there in the worksheet. As long as the amount spent versus the time spent averages about 10% or less, they're most likely doing everything you expect them to do.

How Shoppers Purchase Products

For people you know well, you can give them your business credit card. You can order extra credit cards and authorize others to use them. Close friends and family are great candidates for using your card. You continue to get the benefits of building up points on that card and it keeps your account extremely active which can help raise credit limits in the future as you grow more and more.

Special credit cards for employees do exist but your upside risk is somewhat bad. If they steal anything, limits are often placed on the amount of the theft you can get back. Your regular credit card is better at protecting you from theft by reimbursing you for people who steal from you. You can predetermine a limit that different employees can spend on their employee credit card however. Whereas your credit limit for the card might be $10,000, you can set up your newest shopper's employee credit card with a spending limit of $750 and a shopper who's been with you a while might have a spending limit of $2,500 on the same employee card.

Another way to limit your exposure is to buy gift cards for stores your shoppers shop at. You often can buy them at a discount meaning you might be able to purchase a $500 gift card for Rite Aid Pharmacy but pay only $480 for the $500 face value gift card. You can't cancel a gift card in most instances if you think an employee steals one, but your complete loss potential is often far less than a credit card's limit. Although the employee can take your card and use it, your risk is only limited to the remaining balance of the card at the time of the theft.

If you like the gift card route but a store you're sending a shopper to doesn't have any gift cards, you can purchase Visa gift cards with a preset amount of money on them and shoppers can use those in any store. A drawback of Visa gift cards over most store gift cards is you rarely can purchase Visa gift cards at below face value.

Another way to monitor their spending habits is to use a service called Bento for Business. This allows you to load money onto cards that are basically debit cards. You miss out on some of the cash back that regular credit cards have, but for new shoppers this is a great way to monitor and control their spend. They have to take a picture of the receipt after their shopping trip and load it into the account. Check it out if you want at www.bentoforbusiness.com.

Making a Shopping List

Even before you hire your first shopper, you should be using shopping lists to restock inventory. If you've been happy with the way you create lists for yourself, adapt the same method for your shopper when you hire the first one.

In case you haven't been using a shopping list system, it's well past time but not too late to begin right now.

Use your existing replen tracker (written notebook, worksheet, or replendashboard.com) to see how many replens you need to put on your shopper's list. The number you restock always depends on sales data. For each item needed, enter the following restocking data in a shareable Google Doc:

- ASIN
- Product name
- Amazon link (if possible)
- Cost
- Quantity to buy
- Store name
- Store section/Category

The reason you need a separate sheet for the replens you need (versus your inventory of replens or new replens as they're found) is because your replens tracker will be tracking *all* your inventory including the inventory you don't need to restock yet.

You give shoppers a single, long worksheet of all required buys for the week, separated by store if that works better for you. The separate stores might be a little more efficient for the shopper because they have with them the list of things they need at whatever store they're going to. They won't accidentally buy something at the wrong store because there is a list for a single store.

> **Tip:** You may be curious what the Store Section/Category is in that list. This makes it easier for our shoppers to go to the Grocery section, for example, and buy everything

needed there, then move to the Health and Beauty section, and so on. It also updates in real time so if multiple shoppers are shopping at once, they can see what the other is getting.

You'll appreciate the ease of sharing the same Google Sheet when you have multiple shoppers. As shoppers find products to restock, they can update the quantity. If one shopper only finds 5 but 10 are needed, the next shopper knows to pick up 5 more if they see them.

The Buy Lists

You may wonder why we include the ASIN in the shopper's list. This is to ensure the shopper makes Buy List entries on the correct Amazon listing when using Scoutify or another app. They enter the ASIN into a Buy List and the quantity they bought and other data such as cost.

Your shoppers *must* update the Buy Lists as they find replens. This is true whether a shopper is finding new replens or shopping from a list and adding newfound entries to the Buy List. This ensures the smoothest and fastest transition back at the warehouse when items are ready to prep and ship.

Replen Dashboard App

You'll recall earlier I discussed Replen Dashboard, the software we use to manage our inventory and shopping list creation. If you're at the point where you have graduated from Google Sheets, you'll love this feature of Replen Dashboard. Within the software, when you make your shopping lists, it will automatically send the items you add to a shopping list in the Replen Dashboard phone app. This allows your shoppers to see (in real time) the items you need to purchase, they can enter in the expiration dates, the costs, the amounts they bought, and so much more. In the store, they're able to add these items to a "bought list" so that you can easily create your shipments when they are done shopping by exporting the information and uploading it to your shipment software. Additionally, your shoppers can sort by the Store Category (Grocery, Home, Kitchen, Arts/Crafts, Health & Beauty, etc.)

within the app, making their time MUCH more efficient in the store while shopping. Make sure to check out replendashboard.com when you are at that point in your business where Google Sheets just aren't powerful enough for you.

Getting Back from Shopping Trips

Once a shopper completes a list, he or she brings everything to your warehouse and inputs time and spending amounts into the tracking sheet you saw earlier (or "check in" and input a note into OnTheClock). You or (better!) your warehouse manager tells the shopper which drop-off area to use. This assumes you have more than one inventory drop off area as we do so that you can keep multiple InventoryLab batches open.

Once dropped off, the shopper (or perhaps your designated warehouse manager) sends the Buy List to someone in the warehouse to add MSKUs and upload to InventoryLab.

Shopper Receipts

All shoppers need to scan their receipts into a computer and leave the physical receipt in a folder for you to pick up at a regular time to file away. The scanned receipts enable you to quickly search for a UPC, item name, or store name if there's ever a question about cost or a possible IP complaint is brought against one of the items you sell. The physical receipts serve as the final backup and proof of all purchases.

We use a *Neat* cloud scanner for scanning shopper receipts. By using their cloud service, we can search by UPC or product name for any product and all receipts that include that item pop up. We pay a small amount for the Neat subscription, but you could also store the scanned receipts in Google Drive, Evernote, or Dropbox and access the data that way.

You will need to make sure that the scanner you buy has OCR (Optical Character Recognition) capabilities. This is what allows your scanner to turn the receipts into a readable PDF document so you can search within the receipt later. Many different companies have scanners with this capability such as Epson, Fujitsu, Canon, etc. But each company has scanners without this capability, so it's important to double check before buying one that won't have this feature within the software that's included with it.

VAs – Virtual Assistants

If you know little to nothing about VAs, they can be an extremely helpful part of your business. The reason for their name is you rarely if ever meet them in person. They often live in another country which is one reason you can hire them for such little money, often from $4 to $6 an hour, which is an excellent wage for them.

Tasks VAs Can Do

Tasks that you might hire a VA to do include:

- Find new replens
- Manage your replen list(s) by creating Buy Lists for shoppers
- Manage your Seller Central account by monitoring reviews, returning damaged goods, and fixing stranded inventory
- Open reimbursement cases with Amazon
- Remove unwarranted negative feedback
- Upload Buy Lists to InventoryLab and enter MSKUs for you
- Send emails to query and then set up new wholesale accounts for you
- Look for Private Label (PL) opportunities
- and much more!!

We've never had more than two VAs at a time. Some resellers might hire ten or more VAs. For our replen business, we need only two. We prefer local employees for some of the tasks that other resellers let VAs handle just because we feel we have more control.

Hiring VAs

Many services exist for hiring VAs.

We prefer Freeup (bit.ly/freeupnow). Freeup costs a little more than similar services but they generally require less work to hire people. Freeup takes 15% of the VA's rate (at the time of this writing) which is why they run higher than other services.

The reason we prefer Freeup is we can enter the job description of what we want, whether it's finding new online products or whatever it might be, and they send us a few candidates that meet those job description requirements. We easily can sort through those candidates. Although we pay a little more, there we find good VAs faster who go to work on our tasks quicker.

You can also check out Upwork. Generally, Upwork provides more experienced VAs in various categories, such as logo design work, but they also have general VAs who can do about anything. When you post on Upwork, you'll get a lot of applicants to go through making it a little more hands-on than Freeup.

The most common source for VAs is probably Onlinejobs.ph. Their prices are generally less for the long term because they charge you a monthly fee for using the website, but once you find a VA, you pay the VA directly and no longer pay the website. You'll find many candidates to sift through because the pool is so large and often unspecialized at Onlinejobs.ph. You'll save money but spend more time locating a VA there.

I have some other recommendations specifically for VAs to help you source products and for Account Management to get you money back that Amazon owes you. These are services that already train the VAs for you and give you a service guarantee for their performance, which is unlike any of the other options mentioned above. You can check those services out at askjimmysmith.com/best-resources.

VA Hiring is Simple

When posting jobs, we like to request that the VAs complete a simple task such as putting something in their cover letter to us. It can be silly, such as requesting that they, "Start your response's cover letter to us with the phrase, 'I need a pink Cadillac.'"

You'll know if the applicants read your job description. This is especially important for Onlinejobs.ph where so many send generic responses to newly posted job requests.

Once they pass your first test, ask them to complete a test task based on whatever you will need them to do. You could send them a description of your replen requirements (which you'll have documented by now anyway… right?). Request they find a couple of replens. You could give them a website or two you've used in the past to locate similar replens. Once your candidates complete the test task, you evaluate them and eventually hire.

> **Tip:** Stage Three is when you must be conscious of your operation's details to the point you're documenting every aspect of your business. Your business's scalability requires documentation to grow faster and faster as it gets larger and larger.

Hire two or three VAs for a test period. Give them work for two weeks. At the end of the two weeks, select the one you found to be the best and most reliable.

All this might sound like a lot of work. You want to ensure they can do the basics of the job. This process makes it simpler for you to pull the best VA out of the candidates.

> **Tip:** If the job is one you can benefit from by having two or three VAs, such as finding online replens, hire two or three of the best applicants.

Paying VAs

The pay depends on what you need them to do, but a payment of $4 to $5 an hour works for most tasks you'll hire a VA to do. This includes doing OA, finding replens, or account management. That pay rate is an excellent living wage for many who work for you, most of whom are in countries with a lower cost of living than America's.

We typically pay VAs weekly because unlike employees, making payments is fast and simple. PayPal is about the easiest and best way to pay VAs. PayPal handles required currency conversion for you.

Monitoring Their Time

To monitor a VA's time, we use a service called HubStaff. It costs only $10 per user each month, at the time of this writing. Your VA must sign into HubStaff before working. HubStaff takes screenshots of their computer throughout the day showing you their progress. In addition, HubStaff tracks the hours, minutes, and even seconds they're signed in. Use that to pay them. If you doubt a VA is working the entire time they're signed in, go back and check the screen shots to see if they were working when they said they were.

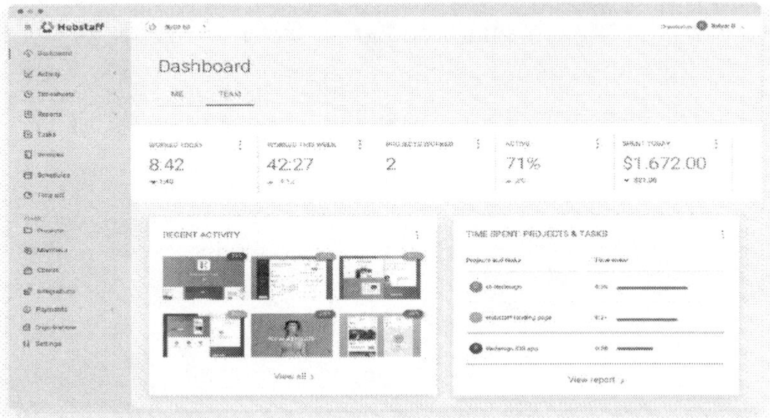

Managing VAs

Always give VAs extremely detailed instructions. Unlike workers physically at your warehouse or shopping for you, a VA can't generally call you throughout the day.

The instructions you give them, with screen shots as necessary, is their primary "training" so you can't be ambiguous. The first time or two you hire a VA, they might have questions you didn't consider or you may have missed a step you should have included. That's great as long as you help them get through that problem *and* you update those instructions for later VAs.

> **Note:** If you send them a video showing how to perform a task, that can be helpful perhaps but it's going to take them longer to master the training. They'll be playing the video, pausing it, and going back to re-watch parts. We find that written instructions with screen shots works best.

Communication is the key. Even though you and your VA won't be routinely speaking to each other, if they have a question they send to you in an email, the faster you (or an assistant) can respond, the faster the VA can get back on the job.

Even though most of your VAs will be in other countries, you will need to speak with them from time to time, more so when they first begin working for you. We prefer Skype for most of these calls, but you can also use WhatsApp or Slack depending on what you prefer.

When they first begin, offer lots of feedback. Give them daily feedback at the beginning and once they get going, send feedback weekly. Offer suggestions, tell them what they do well, and ask them to modify areas where they might not be strong enough.

Finally, require each VA to send you a daily recap email telling you what they accomplished that day, such as, "I found these three replens today." This gives them a chance to let you know if they need something from you and ask questions about problem areas they might run into.

Other Tasks You Can Outsource in Stage Four

Get a general assistant. Our assistant performs a combination of personal and professional tasks including:

- Grocery shopping for our family which ended up freeing up an unexpected amount of time
- Amazon account management
- Manage the Replens List
- Dealing with OA returns and refunds
- Handling refund reimbursements from Amazon
- Managing prep and ship operations

- Creating prep center shipments in InventoryLab that control which of the three drop off tables (or rolling racks if you use those instead) our shoppers work on
- Other random tasks that arise from time to time

Our assistant was our first full-time employee and having a general operations manager like her was a tremendous help for us and our part-time employees.

Consider hiring other tasks you can outsource in your life as well including:

- Lawn care
- Grocery shopping (instead of using an assistant, many grocery services now take care of your grocery shopping)
- Bookkeeping/Accounting/Tax Services (we use Cindy at ecommerceaccountingllc.com since she specializes in eCommerce businesses – which is necessary with the ever-changing rules for online businesses)
- House repairs and car oil changes

If you normally do these kinds of tasks, consider that your time is far more valuable at Stages Three and Four than it was before you began your replens business. Evaluate your time to do these chores and weigh that against hiring somebody to do them.

If you enjoy yard work or you're a gear head who loves working on your car, by all means keep doing the things you enjoy or that relax you. If, however, these and other activities are little more than actual routine chores, outsourcing the work makes complete sense at this stage of the business.

Your time is now worth triple digits. All decisions you make should factor the cost of losing $100+ of value for every hour you mow or grocery shop. Consider ancillary time as well. For example, mowing the lawn requires getting your equipment out before and putting it away after, changing the oil on your gas equipment, winterizing your equipment if you live where winters are cold, buying gasoline regularly to have available at home for the equipment, and so on. Buying groceries might only take you a half hour on the average but you must figure in the drive time to and from the grocery store because that's time you won't be able to work directly on your business.

Discount Gift Card Tracker

At the buying levels your business is at in Stage Four, you no doubt may be purchasing a lot of discounted gift cards from sites such as Raise.com and CardCookie.com. Keeping track of cards, balances, and numbers can be extremely difficult without a system. By now, you know that I want you to be systematizing every aspect of your business, so this won't come as a surprise.

Tracking all your business's gift cards is relatively simple. I created a Google Sheet that lets you track them the same way we do. You'll find the Gift Card Tracking Sheet and all of the other resources for the book here: askjimmysmith.com/bookresources.

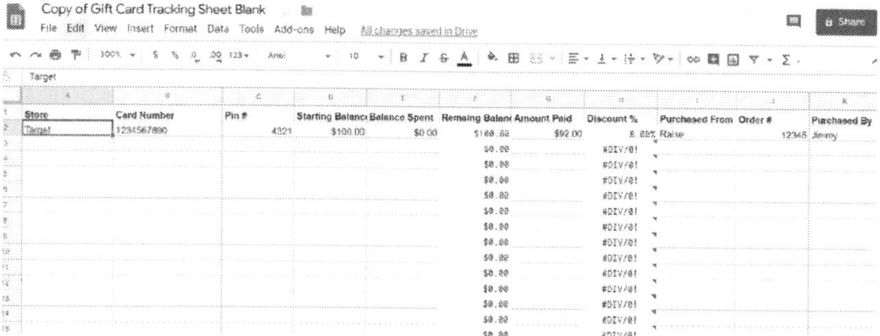

Store	Card Number	Pin #	Starting Balanc	Balance Spent	Remaing Balan	Amount Paid	Discount %	Purchased From	Order #	Purchased By
Target	1234567890	4321	$100.00	$0.00	$100.00	$92.00	8.00%	Raise	12345	Jimmy
					$0.00		#DIV/0!			
					$0.00		#DIV/0!			
					$0.00		#DIV/0!			
					$0.00		#DIV/0!			
					$0.00		#DIV/0!			
					$0.00		#DIV/0!			
					$0.00		#DIV/0!			
					$0.00		#DIV/0!			
					$0.00		#DIV/0!			
					$0.00		#DIV/0!			
					$0.00		#DIV/0!			
					$0.00		#DIV/0!			

The first few columns displayed above are straightforward. They track all your card balances and related data, such as who purchased the card if your VA buys them for you at times.

The remaining columns keep track of other data you may or may not need to track such as how you paid for the card, and random notes that you may want to keep with the card. The final four columns are there in case your card has a balance problem.

If, for example, you purchased a $100 face value card but after spending $47 the balance dropped to zero. You will need to contact the issuing company and begin to resolve the problem and then update these fields:

- NG Card Amount: The amount that went bad on the card, such as $53 (the "Not Good" amount).
- Date: The date you learned the card went bad.
- Resolution: The in-progress or final resolution with the company after contacting them to correct the problem. (These companies often issue another card to you with approximately the same amount or higher or they may refund part or all of your original cost.)

An extremely useful feature appears in the second tab at the bottom of the sheet:

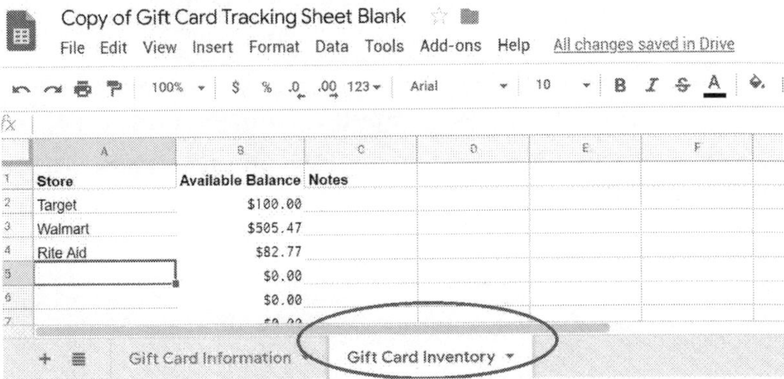

You'll often have multiple cards for the same stores in varying balances. The first screen is where you enter each card and update the information as you add more and spend down the balances. The Gift Card Inventory tabbed screen collects all the data for each store and consolidates everything for that store.

Therefore, if your four gift cards were listed on the first screen, you can click the second tab and type *Walmart* to see the current total balance of all the Walmart cards. This keeps you from having to sort the first screen by store name each time you want to know how much discounted spending power you have at any one store.

Chapter 14

–

Stage Five: Moving from $100,000 to the Stratosphere

You're here – *Congratulations!*

Take time to celebrate but you don't have to *stop* now. There's plenty of growth remaining for you. As a matter of fact, you're now set up to grow far faster and with less effort than at any earlier stage in your journey. Your mindset will focus on growth.

Once you hit $100,000 of sales each month, what then?

By the time you hit $100,000, your entire perspective of business will have changed from the early days of driving to the store hoping to find a replen.

Even truer than ever before, your mindset is the most critical it's ever been. You must shift focus to look forward and plan the following factors:

- How do you want to grow your business from here?
- How can you add more revenue streams that might not all be replens?
- How can you diversify your streams of income (perhaps by creating new bundles, offering Private Label (PL) products, wholesale, utilizing more Online Arbitrage, and so on)?
- Do you need to move to a larger warehouse? (Depending on how you decide to diversify, you may very well need more

space; if, for example, you start packaging your own bundles and PL products, you might need a large area that's not where your company handles replen prepping.)

- Do you add even more employees and continue to outsource as much of the business as you can?
- How can you maximize your cashflow?

Your work ethic is changing fast. You got to Stage Three by grinding and hustling. You got to Stage Five by working smarter, outsourcing work not worth your time, and leveraging your business.

In one way, the grind doesn't stop now or ever if your business grows. The grind is a much higher-level grind and emotionally more rewarding than the old kind of grind. Now, you're thinking in possibilities, shortcuts, bolting on new income streams to the old ones, and considering investment opportunities for your income that aren't all plowed back into your business.

> "Strength and growth come only through continuous effort."
> ~Napoleon Hill

Your work ethic is as critical or more so than it was in the beginning. No business stays even. If you maintain the status quo and don't add new growth opportunities, your business won't stay at $100,000. A strange phenomenon begins to happen. Businesses go down if not fueled with new ideas and new growth. A business never stays even; it grows or shrinks.

Cashflow management is more important than ever because you'll have the same problem you had earlier: too much cash. You must plan what to do with it, perhaps adding more replens, perhaps adding more employees too, and so on.

> **Tip:** I suggest getting a high-level wealth advisor (not "Joe's Money Advice"!) because at $1.2 million dollars in sales and such a small, inexpensive crew working for you, you *are* at a high cashflow level. People you take advice

from going forth must be worth the value you bring to the table. If you go to askjimmysmith.com/financial-protection I'll show you what I do with our money and help you to do the same (free webinar)!

80/20

80% of your time should focus on your current Retail Arbitrage model (assuming RA was mostly responsible for your current sales). Don't let employees think you've lost interest or they will too. Use the other 20% of your time to analyze, test, and implement future streams of income. Your "bread and butter" – the work that got you to this point so well – is the most critical work in your business, so replens are foundational always.

As you work that 20%, finding new streams of income such as wholesale products to resell, you'll now understand why it's critical to approach each new task that works in light of your entrepreneurial mindset and not as a business owner anymore. When Ray Kroc acquired McDonalds #1, the first thing he did was implement a repeatable model that would run without him. He focused on franchising from the start. In a way, you should make everything you do work like a business you can franchise.

By that, I mean document every aspect of your business. When you add new business techniques, document those. Assume you will move to Europe in a week and somebody can step in and run everything without asking you a question. Make yourself dispensable in your own business so you can work more and more on new aspects of it and work less and less on existing aspects.

Someone once said the only reason to own a business is to sell it later. The longer you're the Key Person in your business, the longer it'll be before you can sell your business. And even if selling it isn't your goal, design and grow it as if you'll sell it someday. That is how you maintain the proper entrepreneurial mindset that results in empire building.

Private Label (PL) Ideas

Retail and Online Arbitragers are the best-equipped people to move into PL products (creating products as a brand you own with little to no competition). The reason for this is that we are constantly seeing what products are selling well and we sell A LOT of different products. We are acquiring more data than any other business model for Amazon selling out there.

Too often, items sell well that are on lousy listings with bad photos and hardly any description with bad titles and so on. These are opportunities for you.

Creating new Amazon listings is not difficult. You haven't had to do so with the replen business we've described, but now your opportunities are far better with new capital and a super-powered mindset. Taking a good-selling product on a bad listing and making it a great-selling product on a better listing is surprisingly easy to do once you know what kinds of things sell well (which you know at this level).

You can use your replens to develop private label ideas. It's best to focus on products that sell but are generic, non-brand-driven, and non-electronic (think kitchen scrub brushes and not Apple iPhones). Your experience prepared you to find products that you can source from wholesalers and label them with your own brand.

Often, developing your own private label product literally means hiring a Fiverr designer to create a simple, unique logo for you, hire Staples to print stickers with that logo, finding a few wholesale items such as kitchen scrub brushes that are similar to what currently sell well, dropping your generic brushes into bags or boxes, slapping your logo sticker on the outside, and creating a new listing for your products.

> **Tip:** Many on Fiverr and elsewhere can create Amazon listings for you if you don't know anything about selecting keywords, writing good titles and descriptions, and so on.

Use your RA sales for possible PL ideas. If you've sold good products that get lots of views and sales, items that are generic and non-brand-driven, those are PL opportunities.

Here's how you find any items that might work: In Seller Central, select Reports, followed by Business Reports, Detail Page Sales and Traffic by Child Item. This report brings up a number of pieces of data, including:

- Sessions - this shows traffic
- Buy Box Percentage - how often you get the Buy Box
- Units Ordered - so that you can compare traffic to the number of orders you're getting to get a feel as to how a new product might do
- Total Sales

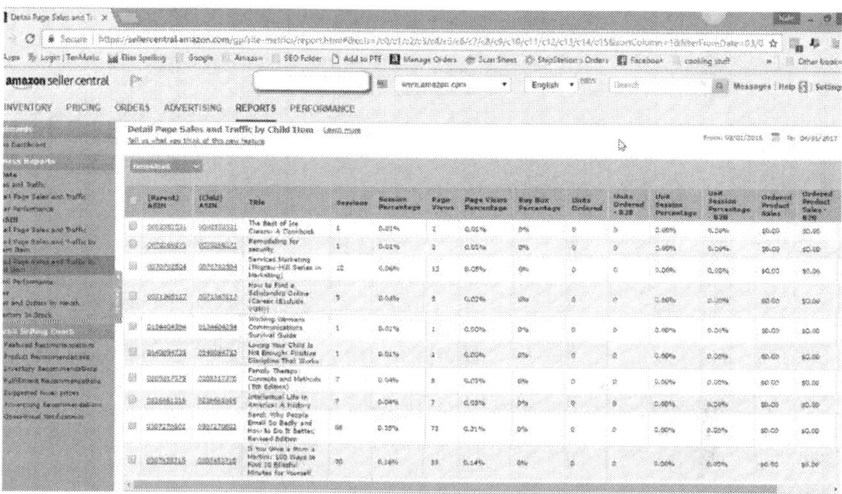

When requesting the report, if you get too much data for a year, narrow down the range to a quarter or so. We sell over 7,000 products each month, so a quarterly report gives us a massive amount of data to analyze.

Filter the report by the most Sessions. This gives you a good starting point to see what's getting lots of potential buyer eyeballs. The more people search for your items the more "sessions" you see. As long as it's not something like a Barbie doll or Roomba vacuum cleaner, but more of a general item like a store-branded item at Dollar Tree for example, you then can look into sourcing it wholesale and putting it in your own package to sell as your PL product.

Even if you don't go the wholesale/PL route, look for opportunities to create bundles from items you regularly sell. You might create a multipack of one of your good sellers or perhaps bundle it with a complimentary product that might make a unique set.

> **Tip:** Make your bundle exclusively yours so that nobody else can sell it. This is simple. Just add a "Tips" or recipe card, such as how to best use the scrub brush or how to make baked goods from the pack of candy or baking item included. The extra card doesn't have to be elaborate. Many people on Fiverr will design it for you. Search the Internet for the tips, rewrite them to work with your item, and send it to Fiverr to design the card. Once you bundle the card and the other product that's already proved to be a seller, nobody can jump on your listing because they won't have access to those 25-cent recipe cards you had Office Depot print up for you!

If you locate a wholesaler that sells a generic version of something that sells well for you, you can almost always brand those kinds of items with your own logo by slipping it into a box or bag with your logo sticker on the outside as I mentioned earlier.

> **Tip:** Head over to askjimmysmith.com/sell-on-amazon to see my favorite, low-risk Private Label course out there!

Whatever route you go, the item or bundled items must be easy to find and continuously available for you to purchase. It isn't worth your time to include in your PL or bundle an item that a store might only stock five of each month.

Low-Hanging Wholesale Fruit

When you follow the previous section's advice to locate private label products, it sort of seems as though you're competing against yourself. You're selling your own PL version of something else you've been selling well. Your new item *could* draw down the other's sales. Don't worry about it. A lot of times, a similar PL product begins to sell with no discernable difference in the other listing. In addition, as your PL items sell more and more, Amazon moves your item higher up in the search results giving you more exposure to new buyers. You'll find that buyers of your PL product aren't the same buyers of the other product.

There's also a way to compete against a replen's other sellers directly. For smaller, lesser-known brands you source to replenish, consider contacting the manufacturer to see if you can become a wholesale supplier. You know how many you can sell through in a year, and by multi-packing and bundling them you could multiply your expected sales greatly. With a good but possible number in mind, the manufacturer might be thrilled to sell directly to you or they may provide a distributor you can open an account with. At worst, they tell you "no" and you still continue buying the products at your retail stores like you did before you contacted them.

In doing this, you no longer pay retail for the item but pay far less. You're now buying wholesale, not retail, and can maintain the same selling price range as before. This enables you to weather dips far better, boost your overall return, and it better ensures you'll never run out of stock. Also, you won't be paying shoppers to source it monthly because you'll just set up an automatic order from the wholesaler or have your assistant place an order when your stock runs low.

Does a Brand No Longer Exist in Your Store?

Wholesalers, manufacturers, and other suppliers lose store contracts or terminate contracts due to cost issues, store demands, and other factors. Once in a while, you'll find such a brand that isn't stocked by any store around you.

Before sending the last one to FBA, look on the package for the manufacturer, contact the manufacturer, and find out if you can purchase items through them. Explain your local situation of being out. We've found new wholesale products to sell this way and we often end up being the only seller on Amazon because other sellers can no longer find the product.

> **Note:** If the product has no company website, look on the product for an address and phone number contact information of some kind. Call them up to make your inquiry.

If you find that a brand is no longer sold in your town or online and you can't find a way to contact the manufacturer directly, all isn't lost. There's likely a wholesale distributor for that product. You'll pay slightly more than you would if you could purchase directly from the manufacturer, but you get to resell the product that's no longer easily found by others. You're likely to end up selling on a listing many other sellers drop off of and never see a new seller get back on. *Sweet!*

Watch for Tanking Prices

Another way to get an exclusive to sell certain products or brands is to keep your eyes out for tanking Amazon prices. The longer prices stay low, the less leverage the brand owner has to keep prices high enough in brick and mortar stores to keep selling it there.

You can contact the brand owner (such as the manufacturer) and explain you're an expert in all things Amazon, that you have a million-dollar reseller business, and you'd like to discuss the possibility of becoming an exclusive, or semi-exclusive, supplier who will guard the pricing and keep the item selling profitably for both you and the supplier.

When you speak to the brand, take the personality of not only a potential seller of their product but also take the attitude you're a friendly consultant who can help them at the same time that they supply you with products.

You don't have to have been selling the item for a long time to research their dipping price trends of course. You have Keepa! Go back six months, a year, two years, and describe those price trends to them. You can send them the Keepa charts as further evidence that you have the proper tools to research brands and prices and you're an expert in doing so on Amazon.

> **Note:** The odds of a manufacturer, wholesaler, or distributor knowing about Keepa are small believe it or not. In most cases, they'll be interested in discussing things further since you have knowledge to research and understand the very thing that's been concerning them: tanking prices and them not knowing what to do about it.

Offer to sell their products on your own account (our preference) or offer to partner up with them on their own Amazon seller account.

> **Tip:** Working alongside a company on their Amazon account to maximize their products' performance while making a good income for both you and the company is an excellent business model. In addition, one of the most important aspects of such arrangements is how you or the company terminate your relationship fairly if things change and they want to handle their own Amazon account by themselves. To see all my recommendations for making money with Amazon, including this business model and wholesale, head over to askjimmysmith.com/sell-on-amazon.

How do You Talk to a Wholesaler?

If you have no experience speaking to manufacturers and wholesalers, you might have some hesitation. Most resellers are surprised how easy it is to talk to wholesalers. Understand those manufacturers and wholesalers want to sell their items as much as *you* want the items to sell to others. To them, you're the customer and they generally never have a combative attitude toward people who contact them wanting to carry their brand or specific products.

To increase your confidence, remember their brand is no longer carried by the stores it used to be carried by (assuming this is the reason you decided to contact them) and they're extra-motivated to locate new companies like yours to sell their items.

Contacting them through email or the phone requires that you adapt a simple script. Change what makes you feel comfortable and add or change any details that needs changing to fit the way you do business. Here's the general script:

> Hello Mr./Mrs. [Name] [or Wholesale Representative],
>
> We're reaching out because we are fans of your brand and know that it would be an excellent addition to the products we carry now. We are interested in purchasing from you in bulk and were curious if you offer large order price breaks that we need to be aware of?
>
> Is there anything you need from me to get us set up in your system?
>
> Thank you!

Asking about large order price breaks tells the company you're possibly a long-term buyer of their products. This sort of script is better at inquiring about wholesale opportunities than simply asking if you can open a wholesale account. You're speaking their language with the large orders and price breaks and you come across as a professional when you mention those.

They'll need your business name and address information along with your reseller tax ID number (FEIN), and possibly more. The worst thing that happens is they tell you "no". But the flip side is you can start an amazing and profitable business relationship!

> **Tip:** Picking up the phone and calling the brand can result in much higher success rates. Brands are getting emails every day from other Amazon sellers that are blasting out mass emails to random brands, so when they get a phone call they are more likely to hear you out. If you do this, be prepared with the data as to why you're calling them (too many sellers on a listing, poor pricing, wanting to help them with their Amazon brand presence, etc.).

Additionally, I suggest adding in some specific information about the brand in that email template. Yes you can send out that generic email, but your results are much better if you differentiate yourself by adding in actual information about their brand (at least have their brand name and some products mentioned that you like.)

Handling Objections from Brands

Be prepared – you WILL get pushback more times than not. This is a good thing! If they just accept anyone that wants a wholesale account, they may not be the best long-term opportunity for you because the competition will rise heavily as other sellers jump on. Your goal is to get them to agree to an exclusive or semi-exclusive relationship. Although, that may be something you push for after your first order if they are accepting any and all sellers instead of trying for it right away.

If you get turned down immediately after asking about opening a wholesale account, it's typically for a few common reasons and most likely they won't just tell you "no" because what business doesn't want more revenue? The thing is, many brands don't like *Amazon sellers* because they don't have a good grip on how to handle the platform, so you will probably be asked if you sell on Amazon, eBay, or other 3rd party platforms. In this case be honest! Let them know that you sell on Amazon and work with brands to help their presence to be controlled on the platform(s). Many times they will respond with, "We already have enough Amazon sellers and don't want anymore."

Since this is a very typical response, you can be prepared for it! I like to respond with this, "Actually, that's one thing I wanted to discuss with you. I usually only like to partner with brands that have less than 3 sellers on the listing since I find that too many sellers reduces the sales price, hurts the branding of the company, and causes confusion among customers. I noticed many of your listings have XX amount of sellers. Is this something that you would like help with?"

This doesn't work every time but it works more often than not to allow you to continue the discussion, which is all you're hoping for at this point. Additionally, you have already begun the conversation of having an exclusive or semi-exclusive relationship.

They may say, "Yes - what can you do?". If you don't know, that's a whole book in and of itself so I can't cover it all here! I recommend either responding with what you would do if you know how to help, or tell them, "There are a lot of different things we can do to help your brand presence on Amazon and to reduce your headaches with the platform. Let's set up a meeting to discuss it so I can prepare some more information on your specific listings for you to review. Would next Tuesday at 2:00 PM Central Time work for you?" This buys you some time to connect in the Facebook groups and get help, to check out one of the courses I recommend, or to watch some Youtube videos for help as well on what you can do to help their brand.

Another objection you may get is something along the lines of, "We already have someone that handles Amazon for us." In that case I usually respond with something like, "Oh I couldn't tell since I saw you had XX number of sellers on your listings and the pricing has varied between $X.XX and $X.XX over the last few months. Would you want to discuss how we can help you with these issues?" Make sure there are more than 3 or 4 sellers and some pricing fluctuation if you do this.

If there is only 1 or 2 sellers and the price is consistent, then you can always check to see if bad reviews are being responded to, if the pictures in the listings are good, if they're using A+ Brand Registered content, if they have a good description and bullet points on the listing, etc. These are other reasons the brand may need your help even if they are using someone else at the moment.

Typically if they have a low consistent amount of sellers with a consistent price, we don't bother reaching out because it's a harder account to get, but sometimes it can be worth trying if you know you can really help the brand.

Lastly, you may find that the brand tells you to contact a distributor of their products because they don't sell direct to anyone. In this case, find out the regional distributor for that brand and contact them. The brand will give you this information freely if they have distributors in place. Distributors will be harder to try to get exclusives with and may not allow any Amazon sellers at all. In this case, move on to a different brand. There are plenty to choose from.

Wholesale is the Most Logical Next Step

Getting to this point in your Amazon business has required a ton of time and effort on your part. You've built an amazing business, scaled, outsourced, and been profitable. That's why wholesale is the most logical next step in your Amazon business journey. You can start this earlier than at this stage if you want, but make sure you don't lose track of your amazing replens business. The best wholesale accounts to get come from those local, regional, and niche replens that you've found in your stores. These companies want and need your help. Nabisco, P&G, and Nike do not need your help. This is all about providing an excellent service for the businesses you work with and these smaller brands need your help to take advantage of the Amazon opportunity that exists.

> **Note:** Smaller brands don't mean a few hundred dollars in sales, they can easily be millions of dollars in sales. One of our wholesale accounts will be doing $50,000 per month between all third party sites as we continue to work with them. So just because I say "smaller brands" that's in comparison to national brands like Nabisco, P&G, and Nike.

If wholesale doesn't interest you, then try Private Label as suggested earlier, any of the other revenue streams below, or simply keep growing your replens business. It is scalable and continues to grow in opportunity!

Add Other Revenue Streams

For the 20% of the time you focus on new revenue streams in Stage Five, here are a few additional ideas to look into:

- Merch – This is a part of Amazon that lets you upload designs for shirts, sweaters, and hoodies and create Amazon description pages for them. You never have to buy one item to sell. Once your design for, say, a ladies V-neck top is up for sale, when buyers purchase, Amazon makes the shirts with your design, ships the V-necks to buyers, and drops the profit to your account. This process is known as *Print On Demand* (*POD*) and is available at merch.amazon.com.

- Books via Print on Demand – Through the Amazon subsidiary known as KDP (*Kindle Direct Publishing*), you can publish your own paperback and Kindle ebooks. As with your Merch account, you don't pay for any inventory or warehouse storage. When a buyer purchases your book, Amazon prints the paperback or sends the Kindle version electronically to the buyer and drops the profit into your account. As with other work you outsource, you can hire writers on Freeup, Upwork, and other sites to write the entire book for you. This often means taking your written or recorded notes and paying someone to turn those notes into a readable book for the audience you want to target. You can learn more at KDP.Amazon.com.
- Consulting/Coaching with companies or individuals who want to learn what you know
- In addition to your Amazon seller account, you can add new reseller channels such as Walmart.com, eBay, Etsy, Mercari, Poshmark, etc.

Chapter 15
–
It's Now Up to You

Your success is in your hands!

By the time you're at Stage Five, there isn't much I can teach you that you haven't figured out already. I welcome your success stories. Please write me any time because I'd love to hear how you took a beginning replen business and built it to 7-figures like so many of my students have since the first edition of this book came out as you can see at askjimmysmith.com/success!

If you are interested in video course content, then the course this book was based on is at askjimmysmith.com/sell-on-amazon or if you want the most comprehensive online selling course out there (which includes my course & many mentioned in this book as well) you can get it at the same link! Additionally, don't forget to get the free jumpstart video training at askjimmysmith.com/jumpstart.

I would really appreciate you leaving me a review at my Amazon book listing for *Side Hustle to Full Time Income* at amazon.com.

Be sure to follow me on Youtube @AskJimmySmith, Instagram @AskJimmySmith, or at my website for regular blog and video content at askjimmysmith.com.

~ Jimmy Smith

Feel free to email me at jimmy@askjimmysmith.com if you have any questions or need to reach me for anything.

You'll find all additional resources for this book at askjimmysmith.com/bookresources

Made in the USA
Middletown, DE
25 October 2023

41393490R00146